Sixty Days Under The Influence

A Photo Journal Through France

BILLY CONE

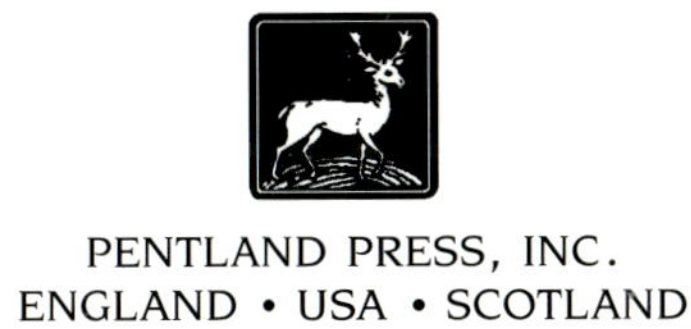

PENTLAND PRESS, INC.
ENGLAND • USA • SCOTLAND

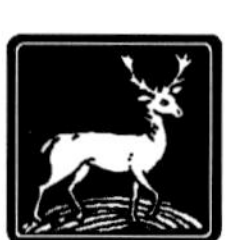

PUBLISHED BY PENTLAND PRESS, INC.
5124 Bur Oak Circle, Raleigh, North Carolina 27612
United States of America
919-782-0281

ISBN 1-57197-064-9
Library of Congress Catalog Card Number 96-65961

Hexagon Books

Printed in Hong Kong

I'd like to thank my mother, Emily, *for the idea to create this book and for her inspiration and endless enthusiasm.*

Sixty Days Under The Influence

A photo journal through France

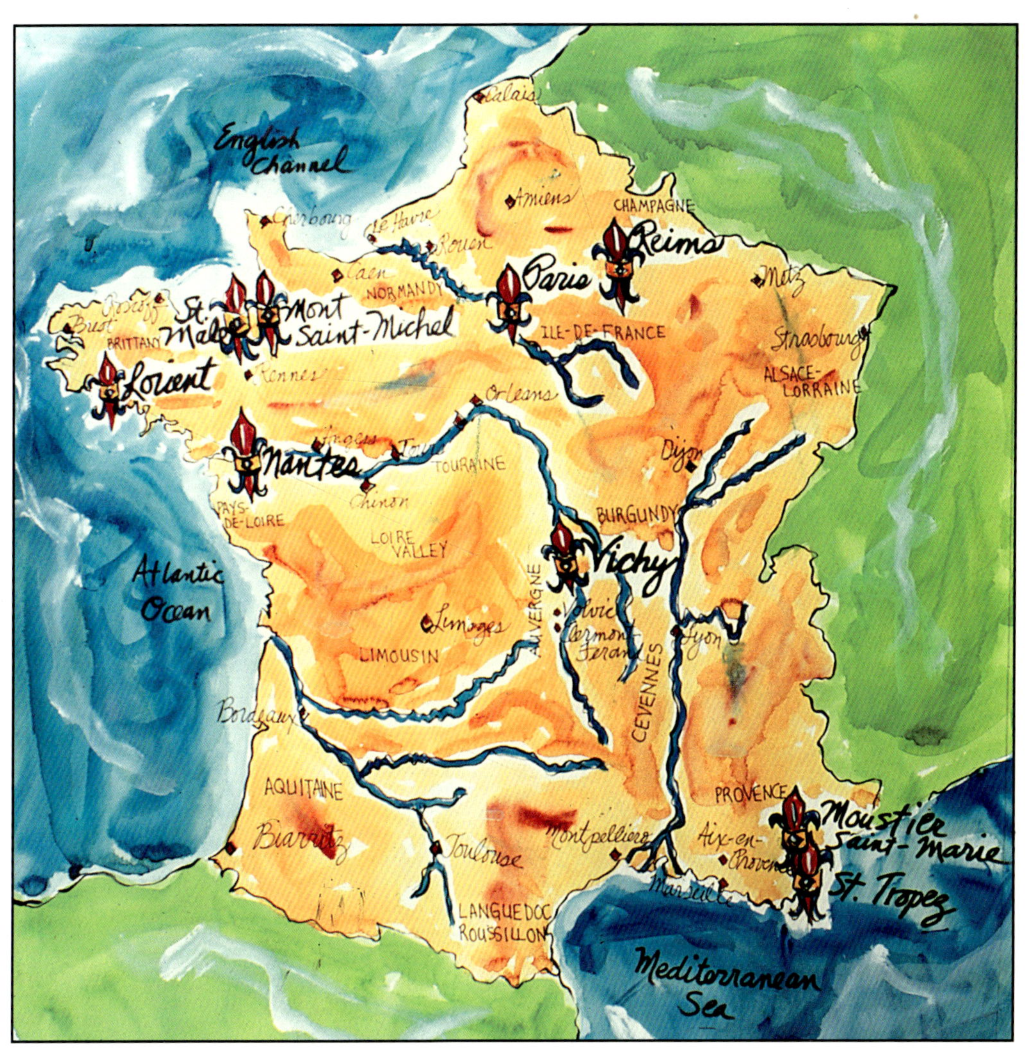

Map painted by artist, Deborah Cavenaugh,
a resident of Wilmington, North Carolina

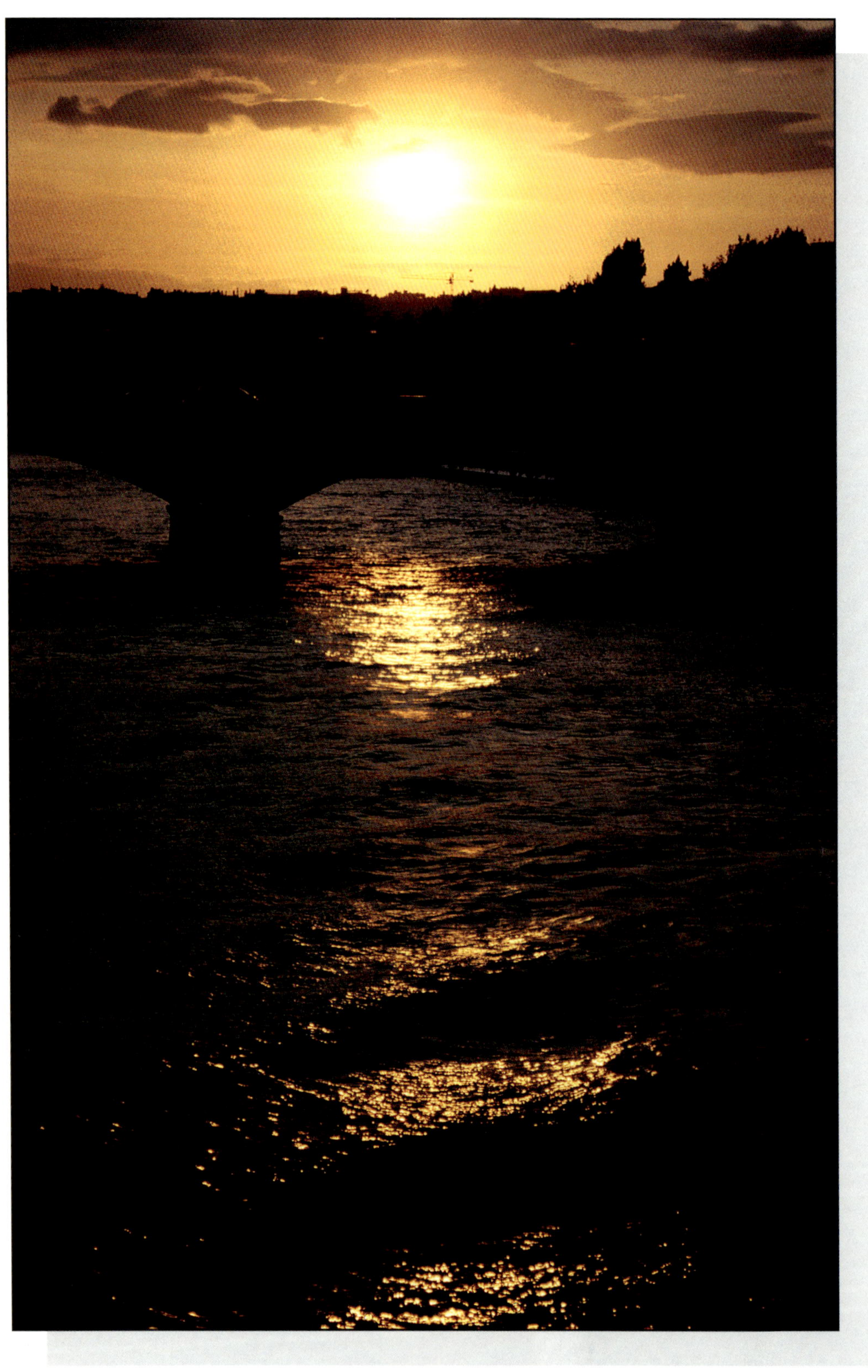

The sun sets and shines on the city's life blood, the Seine River.

Introduction

France, known throughout the world for producing the finest wines known to man, is intoxicating for many other reasons. My love affair with the country and the language began in 1983, when I lived with a French family and attended school in Vichy. That *séjour en France* (sojourn in France) lasted ten months, as I took a road trip to Saint-Maxime with two *Vichissoises* (women from the town of Vichy), spent *Noël* (Christmas) with Philippe and Véronique in Vichy, left Aix-en-Provence to go to school in the less-touristy town of Grenoble, got a job working in a *patisserie* (pastry shop) there, moved to Paris to work in the bakery at Fauchon, and had my car stolen and later retrieved. Ever since that first trip, I have been keeping detailed journals of my visits to this land of beautiful countrysides, quaint little villages, antiquated dwellings, majestic monuments, flower-filled gardens, winding rivers, and a gastronomy that ranges from simple to complex and often achieves the sublime. I have found the culture to be a living entity which has continued to grow and enrich itself since the time of the *Gaullois* leader Vercingétorix, who, even though defeated by the Romans in 52 BC, is remembered today as a popular cartoon character named Astrix. There are too many aspects of France to mention all of them here in this short work, but I must speak about the glue that binds these people and all other Francophones together—the language. Unlike any other nation in the world, France has an organization, called the *Academie Française*, created solely to protect the integrity of the language. Its forty members with diverse backgrounds are the most erudite and eloquent speakers and writers in the land, and maybe in the world. In fact, the French language is really the people's religion, their God.

In the following pages, I write about my recent photographic trip to France, on which I studied the language in Paris while living with a French family; visited friends in Nantes, Lorient, and Vichy; and journeyed to the border of Brittany and Normandy to Le Mont Saint-Michel, down to Saint-Tropez where I met a wonderful person, then to a truly culinary capital called Provence, and finally back to the City of Light for a few more exciting days of discovery and photography. As you will discover, food is a meaningful thing to me, and I try to give detailed explanations of the kinds of meals I enjoyed along the way. Although this is not a guidebook, there are plenty of ideas for the traveler who needs to know of a restaurant or a café or even a hotel here and there. I suggest that to get the most out of this journal you imagine being there as you focus on the pictures and let the writing entertain you and give you the flavors of France and its culture. The format is exactly that of a journal or diary, only it was written for you, *le lecteur* (the reader), with colorful photographs to help you get in the proper frame of mind. Enjoy!

Paris, dimanche et lundi 30 avril et 1 mai

Paris, Sunday & Monday, April 30th & May 1st

Kennedy was chaotic as usual until I arrived at *Le Club*, where I could help myself to drinks and nabs and where I knew I was on my way to France when I saw a couple with a huge dog in the lounge. Soon in the plane, I found myself pressed to my seat and we were defying the ground below. Leaving the gloom of Gotham behind, we climbed and climbed until we were spit from the turbulent gray through a giant coverlet of zillions of cotton formations into the pale blue, flying away from the setting sun. With a new-found sensation of peacefulness, I sank into my leather chair and stared back at the color-filled sky until another glass of champagne was put before me. I was in my element—traveling. But not just traveling—France was my destination, and I was flying on frequent flyer miles in the business section in the upper deck of an Air France 747 jumbo jet.

My neighbor's name was Hanele, and believe it or not we played the game where you try to guess each other's name. Hanele! I could have guessed for weeks and I would never have said Hanele. But I did guess that her name started with an "H" on my very first try. Hanele was impressed. She was of Finnish descent, and she and her husband were on their way to the Alps, not for pleasure, but for her father-in-law's funeral. They seemed to be doing well under the circumstances.

In the meantime, a French flight attendant wined and dined us all the way to Charles DeGaulle Airport, where we landed twenty minutes ahead of schedule. Impeccable service!

At the suggestion of the family I would be staying with, I got on the Roissy Bus headed to *Place de L'Etoile* at the *Arc de Triomphe*, and could sense it in the air that I was in France—someone was smoking! Forty-five minutes later, my bags and I got off, and we began searching for *rue du Faubourg Saint-Honoré*, which was easy enough to find, only I went down the wrong avenue, so I was twice as far away as I would have been had I taken *Avenue Hoche*. Even worse, I went in the wrong direction until I realized that #225 was about twelve blocks the other way. My arms were about to fall off, I had jet lag, and I needed sleep.

Finally I arrived, and after ringing every doorbell on the second floor, a cute little woman in her forties and her younger brother opened the door and showed me to my room. We spoke for a while and they told me that things had been a little confused there since the death of their mother in January, but they were

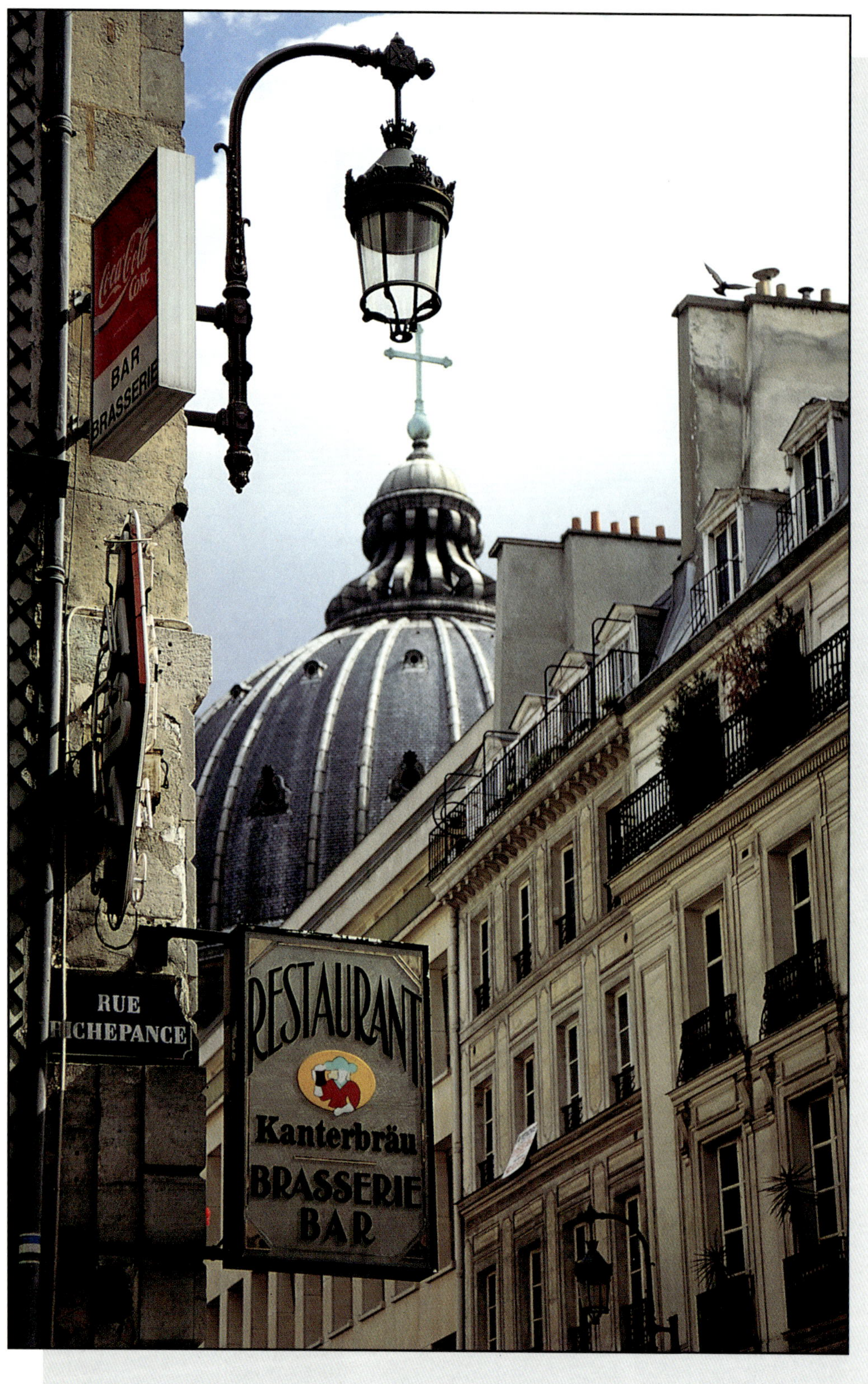

The corner of rue Richepance and rue Saint-Honoré.

now back to their old established routine of living. Madame Marchand had been housing foreign students since 1960, all the way up until the day she died. In fact, even with all that going on, there was never a time when no *locataires* (lodgers) were staying in the home.

Both of her children, Jeanne-Marie and Gilbert, have traveled extensively and speak some English. However, no English would be spoken here, fortunately for serious students of French.

Why does everything edible seem to taste better in France? It's true! Ask anyone who's been there. After some super tea with creamy Normandy milk, I crashed till about 17h00.

This day in France was a holiday, similar to our Labor Day, the one day a year that young people sell sweet-smelling white flowers called *muguets* (lilies of the valley) along *trottoirs* (sidewalks) in cities all over the country.

Ternes was the closest *métro* (subway) to the apartment, so I caught it there and headed to *Saint-Germain des Près*, where I walked a few blocks to Le Procope, a restaurant opened in 1686 as a simple coffee shop, making it the oldest restaurant in the world. I had a *Kir Royal* (*champagne* and *creme de cassis*), some little meat *terrines* as *hors d'oeuvres*, grilled filet of sole in a lemon cream sauce with the first baked potato I'd ever been served in France, and an endive salad with Roquefort cheese. Something to remember here in France: If you desire just a glass of wine in a restaurant, it will often be a coarse *Côte du Rhône* or something of much lower quality than what is offered in bottles. There are exceptions, but the best plan is to order a half bottle if you want a small quantity of good wine.

Anyway, the food was good, even though the wine could have been better, and for dessert I had *profiteroles*, which are puff pastries filled with vanilla ice cream and covered with hot chocolate sauce. For some reason (maybe I lived here in another life), I have always felt at home in France, even by myself. *Bons rêves* (Sweet dreams)!

Paris, mardi 2 mai

Paris, Tuesday, May 2nd

I slowly got out of bed, and had some hot tea with milk and a *tartine* (a buttered slice of *baguette* with jam). Even a shower was not enough to fully wake me, so on my way to shoot I stopped at a *café* called Le Hoche and ordered *un café* (espresso), which not only got the blood rushing but also improved my French, because I was totally aware of what people were saying around me when I overheard their conversations. Careful with this wonder drink!

I remember my first trip to Paris most by the very first day I landed, when, at one in the morning, I drank my very first espresso and was wide awake staring at the ceiling and cracking jokes with my friend all night long.

One of my favorite places to take photos is on and around *Le Pont Alexander* III, which was built around the turn of the century, so I headed there and found that I was not the only photographer with this idea. An older gentleman from

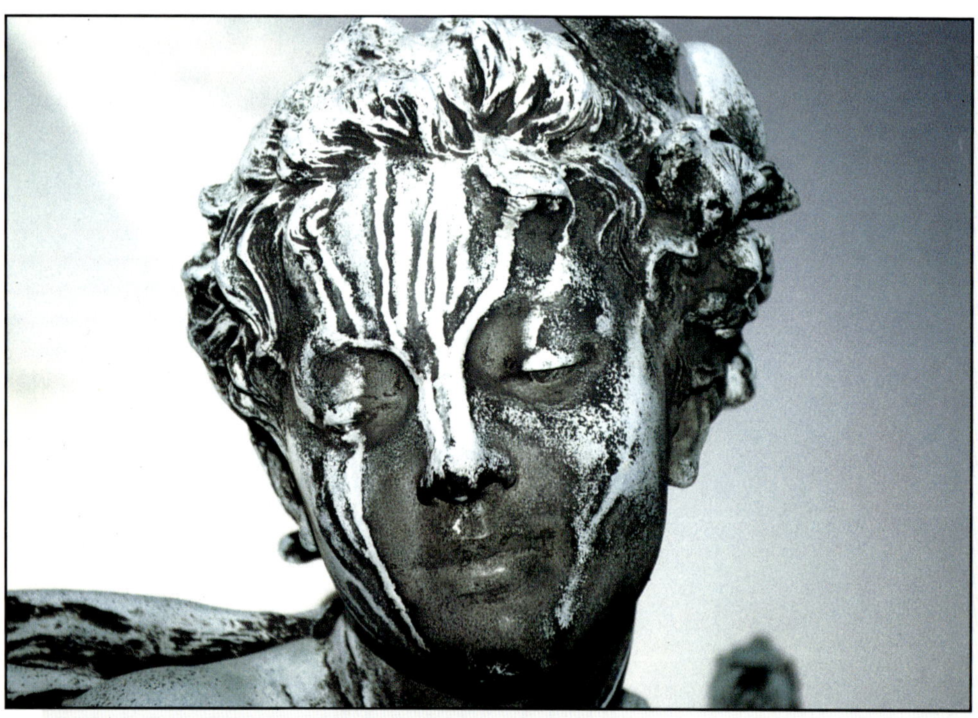

A heavenly bust on the Alexdander III bridge.

Australia, with a tripod, two cameras around his neck, and one in his hand, looked like he was pacing the *trottoir* of the bridge hunting for that perfect *cliché* (picture). Gee, all I have is a Nikon F4, a 28-85 Nikkor lens, a trusty circular polarizing filter, and a flash, but that's all I really need. I didn't want to be late for my first day of school, so I took one last picture of one of the many angelic statues found on both sides of *le pont*.

The *responsables* (administrators) of L'Institut de Langue Française put me in the next-to-highest level, and my first day was very interesting, because my teacher spoke about the origin of the city of Paris. It turns out that in 32 BC, Lutèce, the city's first name, was born on what is now the Ile de la Cité. Julius Caesar called the people of Lutèce *Parisii*, and that is where the name Paris came from. The Romans later settled on the Rive Gauche, which is why it is called the Latin Quarter today. When Christianity became the predominant religion, the Temple of Mercure and the Temple of Jupiter were replaced by *Le Sacré Coeur*, perched on Montmartre, and *Notre-Dame* respectively. Ironically, the uninhabited *Ile aux Vaches* (Island of Cows), which was cut off from the *Ile de Notre-Dame* by Charles V to protect the city, is now the *Ile Saint-Louis*, the most expensive residential real estate in France today.

I also learned the origin of the word "bistro." When the Russians occupied Paris, they used to frequent restaurants around Montmartre, where they would go in large groups, and while waiting for their food they would get impatient and yell, "Bistro, Bistro!" To the French this word meant "*vite*," or "hurry up." Speaking of bistros, I ate dinner at Le Bistro Roman on the Champs Elysées, one of a chain of reasonably priced *restos* around Paris where the Italian raw beef carpaccio seems to be the most popular *entrée*. The French love raw meats and raw oysters, and if the meat is cooked, it's usually *saignant*, or barely singed on both sides, blood red in the middle. Not for me!

I had tomatoes and mozzarella with olive oil; *margret de canard*, slices of duck breast with the delicious fatty skin surrounded by a semi-sweet cassis sauce; and green, herby fettuccini noodles. Early to bed after some *devoirs* (homework). *Bonne nuit à tout le monde* (Good night everybody)!

Paris, mercredi 3 mai

Paris, Wednesday, May 3rd

Wow, is it beautiful here, with such gorgeous weather, and I was told that it had rained for two weeks straight before my arrival. What can I say? I brought some good ol' North Carolina weather with me.

Today I took my "traveling companion" to *Parc Monceau*, a small park of flower gardens, manicured bushes, and trees; of course it is *de la pelouse*, which is "off limits" even for sunbathers or picnickers. What a drag, but I guess there wouldn't be much grass if everybody used it. Such are *les grandes villes* (big cities)! It's very near where I live, and is one of the places where mothers and baby sitters bring children of wealthy families that live near the *quartier* to stroll and play. After taking some pictures and walking around the oval dirt path that begins on the *Arc de Triomphe* side with a beautiful gold and black gate and goes around two other similar entrances to ruins and a pond on the other end, I headed to class.

My teachers were excellent. Michele explained everything and answered all of our questions, and my literature *professeur*, Christelle, was thorough, friendly, attractive, and single. My fellow classmates came from Japan, Jordan, Sweden, Germany, Argentina, Columbia, and Italy. It was quite a diverse group, and fascinating to hear about each other's countries and customs.

At 16h15, I caught the *métro* to Saint-Paul, where I walked to *La Place des Vogues*, the heart of *Le Marais* district. I really loved the way the trees were cut inside the *place*, all neat and squared-off like giant green boxes encircling the garden-like interior space. I walked to Saint-Michel and had a beer in a café in which a dog and a cat were just hanging out together in harmony. Either they were extremely well-behaved or they had already eaten that day, because they couldn't have cared less that customers were eating. I love that about France, because it's so French. But on the other hand, I'm glad that animals are *interdits* (prohibited) in restaurants in America. In this country, dogs and cats are kings and queens, and the French take them to the store, to restaurants, and even to work. Heaven help the man who gets caught being cruel to an animal in France! They probably still have some *guillotines* left somewhere just for that crime.

When I had finished drinking my Leffe, a somewhat-sweet *blonde*, I worked my way to the *apart* to relax and read before dining at the *bistro* of the four star Hotel Lutetia, not to be confused with the extremely expensive restaurant inside the hotel itself. I downed a couple of *Kir Royals* while I waited for my tomatoes stuffed with caviar of eggplant, a food for the gods. Then the *serveur* brought me the steaming hot *casserole* of cabbage leaves stuffed with ground veal, lamb, beef, and tantalizing spices. My food was not the only thing stuffed that night, but I, being a *gourmet*, or *gourmand* if you like, had to try the *creme au chocolat*, a really thick mousse of pure dark chocolate that melted in my mouth. Just so you'll know, a *gourmand* is someone who loves to eat almost anything, often in fairly large quantities, and a *gourmet* likes to eat fine foods from around the world.

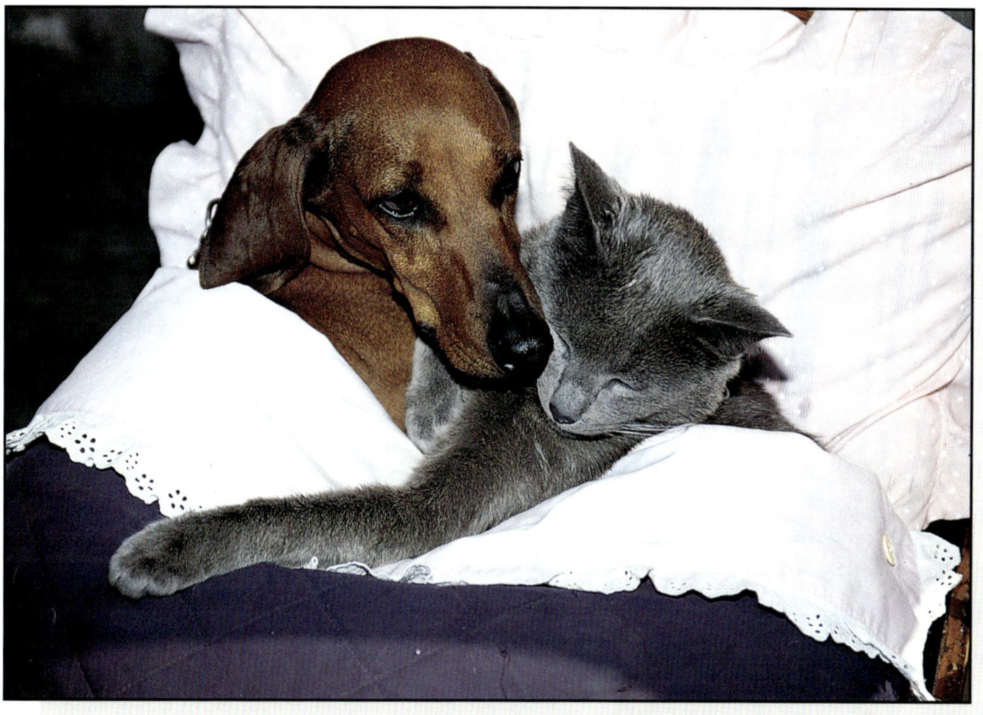

A not so uncommon sight in France-canine and feline harmony.

Paris, jeudi 4 mai

Paris, Thursday, May 4th

Turns out that I could have and should have bought a one month *carte orange* (orange card) for the *métro*, which allows you to use all the subways and buses for that period of time, but now it is too late to benefit from one. The Paris RATP has other *cartes* (cards) valid for several days to a week or even a year that you should consider if you are going to use the transportation system often. I usually just buy a *carnet* (booklet) of ten tickets which can last a week or two days depending on how much I need to zip around beneath the city.

This morning I went to *Le Sacré Coeur* and took pictures in the beautiful morning sunshine and all-too-familiar haze of Paris. Then I walked a long way to the currency changers on the rue du Rivoli to change one grand in order to pay my family. The rate, 4.78 francs to the dollar, was a slight improvement over the rate at *L'Office de Tourisme*. I remember when the dollar was worth over ten francs back in 1984. When changing money in Paris, understand that wherever you go will have a different rate, and it would seem that some changers are downright *voleurs* (thieves), because the rate they exchange is far from the current rate established by the banks. Beware of this! Know the current established rate for comparison, and also know that the more money you have to change the better the rate should be. Commission is usually built into the rate, so don't be fooled by a *bureau de change* (exchange bureau) that says "No Commission."

I took the *métro* home to get books and was off to class. My teacher gave me the idea to visit a not-so-well-known park near the University of Paris called *Parc Montsouris*. She said that this beautiful place was near her home and that it was often overlooked by photographers, so how could I resist? After an expensive taxi ride all the way across town, it quickly became apparent to me what my teacher was talking about. I found a beautifully-manicured green bastion of tranquility protected by tall trees from the moving cars and the brick and mortar all around. I took many *photos*, and when I came upon a small *crêpe* vendor, I couldn't resist one with sugar and a Perrier.

Some boys were trying to retrieve a white ball from the pond by throwing dirt and rocks from the opposite side, but the wind kept the ball away from the bank. It's amazing how children have such hopeful enthusiasm when faced with such a problem. But I can remember being that way too. When I was very young it was like my life was a movie and there was always many people watch-

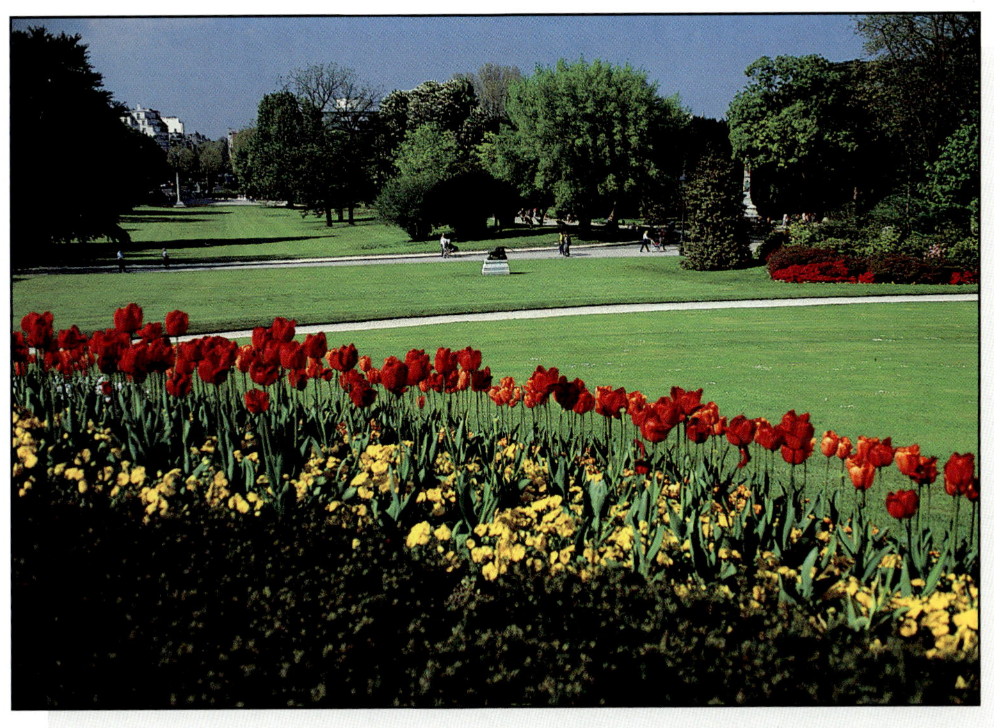

The lesser known park of Montsouris located south of the center of Paris near the Cité Universitaire.

ing and I was performing for them with cool confidence. That's how I remember my youth.

Later, I explored the university campus while African music resounded from the woods nearby. What was once foreign is becoming familiar.

I caught the RER train to *Charles de Gaulle Etoile* and then the #2 in the direction of Nation to Ternes, where I walked a block to the Marchand's. For dinner we had a *salade niçoise,* a hamburger with a sunny-side-up fried egg on top, a little "sandy" *rosé,* and coffee ice cream for dessert. The French like to say, "*Métro, Boulot, Dodo*" to explain their day. Today I feel the same way: "Subway, Work, Sleep." A *demain* (See you tomorrow)!

Paris, vendredi 5 mai

Paris, Friday, May 5th

After paying a visit to a *pharmacie* and buying a book and some music at the FNAC, I went to a *traiteur*, a sort of French delicatessen with all sorts of wonderful gourmet prepared foods to take out. From among the dozens of salads, I chose one with shrimp, corn, and cucumbers, and another with big beautiful artichoke hearts in a French vinaigrette sauce. Just two doors down I bought a *demi-baguette* and my favorite non-alcoholic drink besides Coke, Orangina; I took my "picnic lunch" home and ate it in the kitchen—delectable and light!

Eleanor, the *bonne* (housekeeper) from Martinique, was cleaning and cooking when I met her. She was very nice. Since I often get a little excited when meeting strangers, she was kind enough to teach me how to approach French women in public. You have to be cool and have confidence, she said. Oh, that's all it takes! *Plus facile dit que fait* (easier said than done).

After class, I took the *métro* to the *Ile Saint-Louis*, where I took a lot of pictures. I went to *Notre-Dame* and walked along gallery-filled streets and took the *métro* home for dinner. We had gratin of fish and mushrooms, gratin of eggplant, and sauvignon wine. We joked and laughed about the current presidential election between Lionel Jospin and "my man" Jacques Chirac, and *Gilbert et moi* planned to open a *crêperie* in the U.S. All I had to do was call him and he would come from his home in Australia to help me—right! But it's fun to plan, anyway. Who knows?

Later that night, Miriam took me to a party given by one of the Greek students at school. It was pretty far away from the center of Paris, on the twenty-first floor of a modern high-rise. The party was a little boring for me, so I left and caught the very last *métro* home at 12h46.

On my way from the station I came upon a *mendiant* (homeless beggar), who wasn't begging but had passed out on the sidewalk, and I had this sudden rush of an idea to give him a "Eugène Delacroix" (equivalent to an "Andrew Jackson"). When he opened his swollen eyes, he was almost in shock at my gesture. Later, I wondered what good that would do him, and it depressed me to think about how much money and love it would take to get someone like that back on his feet in society. It's almost a no-win situation and certainly an ugly commentary on our welfare systems. *Au lit* (off to bed)!

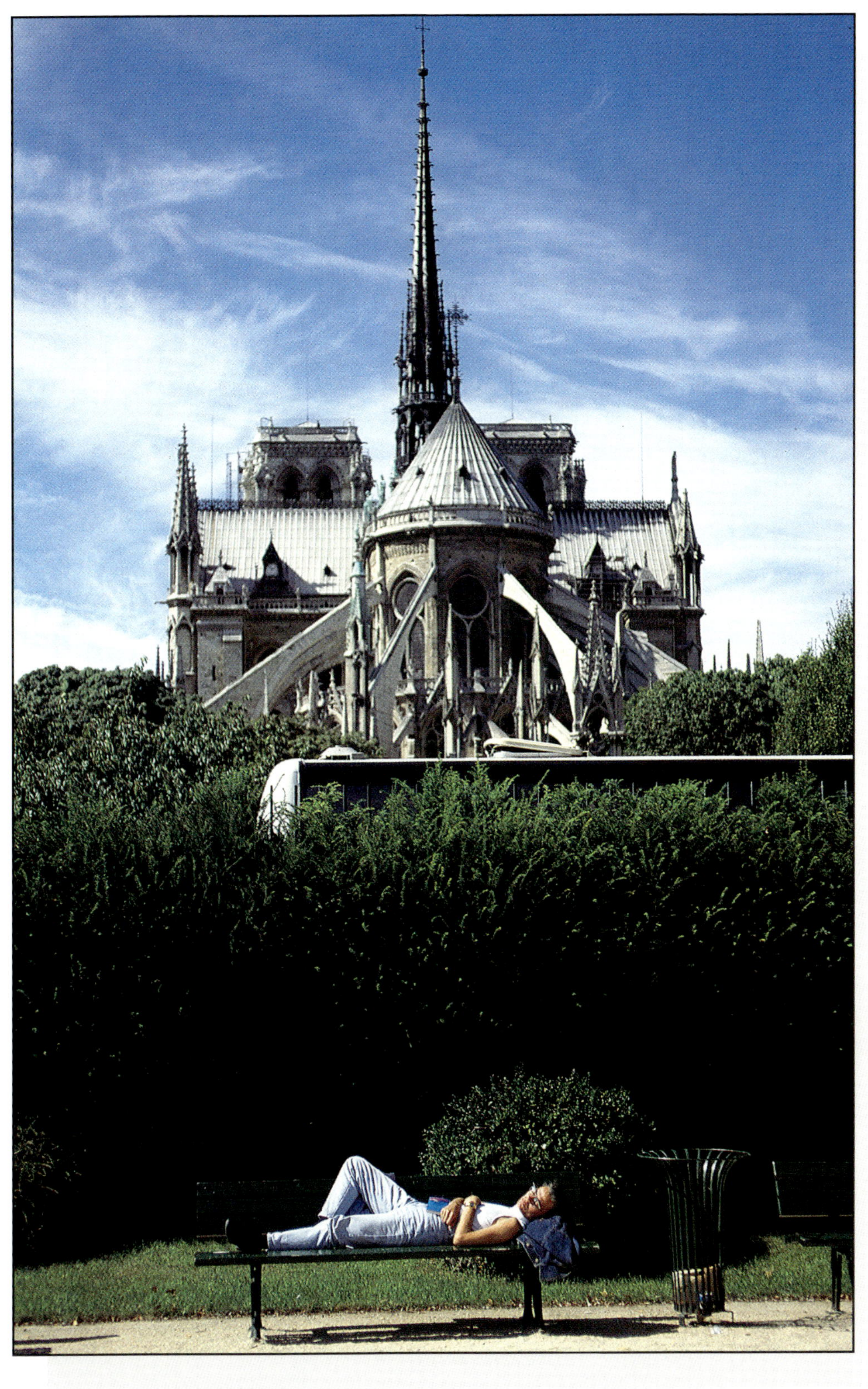

Behind Notre-Dame, in a secluded little park,
is a peaceful place for a nap.

Paris, samedi 6 mai

Paris, Saturday, May 6th

I went to the perfectly laid out Luxembourg Gardens and walked around taking photos, ending up at the lesser-renowned department store called *Au Bon Marché,* where I caught the subway home from *Sèvres-Babylone. Au Bon Marché,* which offers quality merchandise at more reasonable prices than some of its competitors, and has a wonderful *épicerie* (grocery) where you can shop for already-prepared lunches and dinners, is one of the oldest department stores in Paris.

For lunch we had Guadeloupe chicken and quiche in the kitchen and had an enjoyable forty-five minute coffee afterwards. At times like these we would just talk French about *n'importe quoi* (anything). It was great! Later, Gilbert and I supplemented our coffee buzz at a nearby café, and then I went to the *Prisunic* (another chain of stores that has an *épicerie* and general merchandise) to buy the wine for Sunday.

When I got home I changed and went to the *Mosquée de Paris, Le Jardin des Plants,* and McDonald's for some *champagne américain,* Coke. *McDoe's* is one of the few places to get a Coke with a reasonable amount of ice, a rare commodity in France. I sat down with an eighteen-year-old French girl and started a conversation when a poor street person walked in. She was very peaceful but somewhat at the end of her rope, so the girl I was with gave her fifty francs in food stamps. The woman was grateful and immediately bought a meal. She ate slowly and savored every bite. I felt good, and I felt bad. Where would her next meal come from? I slipped her a fifty franc note as I was leaving, and at this point she was glowing at her good fortune. It's confusing! In a city like Paris I never know in my heart whether to help these people, and if so, how much to give them when I do. I guess I just react when I feel moved, and maybe that's enough. The musicians in the *métro* need a break, but I have a personal rule never to reach for money in subways or in a crowd. That would be asking for trouble.

I left the McDonald's and went walking along the left bank of the Seine, taking many photos of the art installed along the river, and of the dogs and boats. I've decided to do a book on Paris with short writings to sell here in France first and then *ailleurs* (elsewhere) like in the U.S. I have to live here—it's in my blood. When I had no more film left, I walked to my favorite *resto,* Le Procope, and had an *Américano*—Campari, Martini Rosso, lemon and orange slices, and ice—for an *apéro*; lobster from Canada; oysters the size of oranges; *vin rouge* (red wine); and, once again, *profiteroles* of homemade vanilla ice cream and hot chocolate sauce. Yes—incredible how good I can be to myself sometimes!

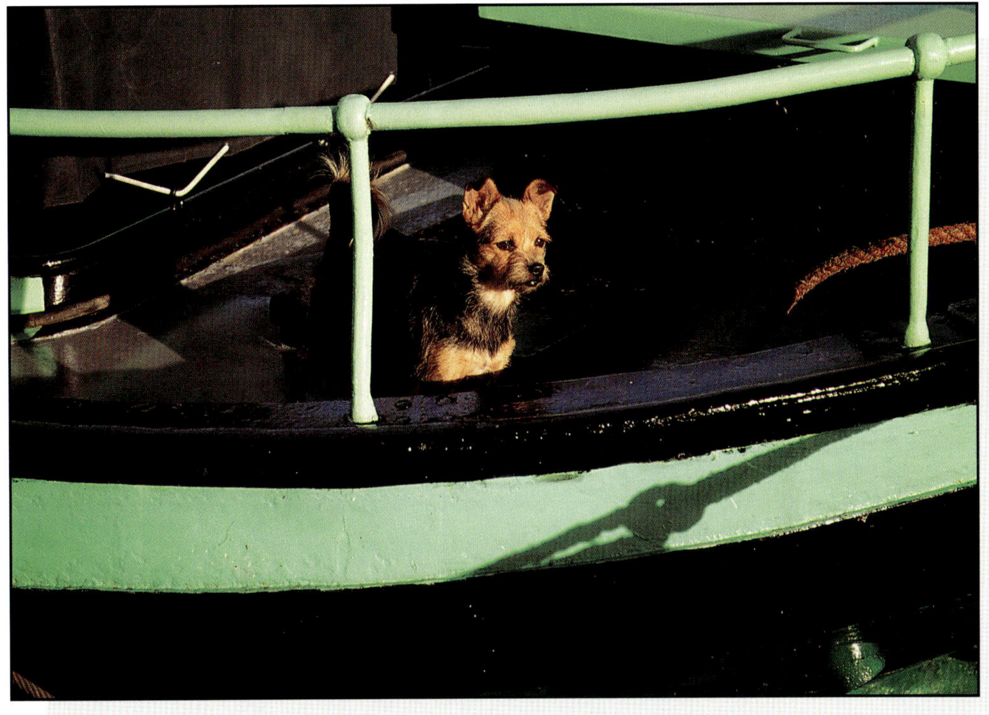

In France, dogs and cats rule.

My dreams inspired by this country are ever present, and almost everything here reminds me to believe in them. At the magazine stand, some young people were trying to help me figure out when the next Bulls playoff game would be. They told me *mardi* (Tuesday), and so my Tuesday was planned. First, I would go to the fashion show at Printemps, then class, then to hear Isaac Stern, and then to some bar that has television with *Canal Plus* (a private television station, sort of like ESPN, but with feature films and other programming as well as sports). *C'est tout* (that's all)!

Paris, dimanche 7 mai

Paris, Sunday, May 7th

Today I went to *messe* (mass) at *Notre-Dame* Cathedral, and to get in, I had to maneuver around all these barricades with *flics* (cops) everywhere. I stopped to ask one why I couldn't enter, and he responded, in French, "There are celebrities in the church today." *Je m'en fou moi* (I don't care), I thought, I'm getting in. And I did, along with thousands of other people who were already seated. I sat down, but for the rest it was standing room only. The service was beautiful, and if you didn't get inside you could have watched and listened to the large television screen just outside of the church. Progress!

Next, I went to *La Gare Saint-Lazare* to check times and buy a ticket to go to *Bois Colombes*. Hunger was striking, so I walked to *Fauchon*, which was closed, so I opted for *Angelina*. There, it was pleasant except for a homeless drunk who came in and ordered wine, and they served her, of all things. She couldn't pay, so there was a scene. Then a middle-aged lady near me offered to pay for everything except the booze, but she hadn't ordered any food, so this kind lady paid anyway. The drunken woman in rags came over to thank the stranger, and she smelled awful. All around me people were motioning towards *la porte* (the door), but she went back to her original table, and fortunately for the *salon de thé* (tea room), no customers left. *Alors* (usually means "Well" or "So," but can mean other, non-translatable expressions), it wasn't over. The police arrived with their paddy wagon, and at just about the same moment, our friend decided to come back to speak with the generous lady, threatening to "stink" up my section of this very fine establishment. *Entrent les flics* (enter the cops), who gently carried her off, with a little protesting, in *le panier à salade* (paddy wagon). This is what's sad about *les grandes villes*.

While this was all going on, I was having a nice conversation with a lovely French-Japanese woman. *Normalement* (it means "normally" or "usually," but when the French say it, it most often means "normally, except in this case"), *Angelina* is packed at this time of day, so I asked the French-Japanese woman where everyone was. She said that for the last five years the quality of life has gone down in Paris and that people were spending less money. After a delicious salad, and a "Mont Blanc" made from meringue, *chantilly* (whipped cream), and chestnut cream, and a coffee, I walked several miles home and shot pictures.

At the house, I grabbed my wine and worked my way back to *La Gare Saint-Lazare* to catch the train to Thierry and Karine's for the grand occasion of their *crémaillère* (housewarming party), on the night of the presidential election. Fortunately, Jacques Chirac won. I've wanted this former mayor of Paris to be president since I lived in Vichy in 1983. I was happy, and we all celebrated, first with incredibly strong punch, then *rosé* wine, then red, then *champagne*, and finally some kind of after-dinner brandy. The French really have a special way of loosening the tongues of foreigners with so many different kinds of spirits! My friends drove me back into the heart of the city to *Place des Ternes*, and I was home. As a passenger, I find that nocturnal Lutèce has tremendous visual appeal with all of its street lamps, the rows of old buildings, and late night cafés lit up like Christmas trees. At night, the ultimate drive would have to be around the *Arc de Triomphe*, down the *Champs Elysées*, and past the *Petit* and *Grand Palais* to *La Concorde* and around the *orangerie* and up the *rue de Rivoli*. *Salut*!

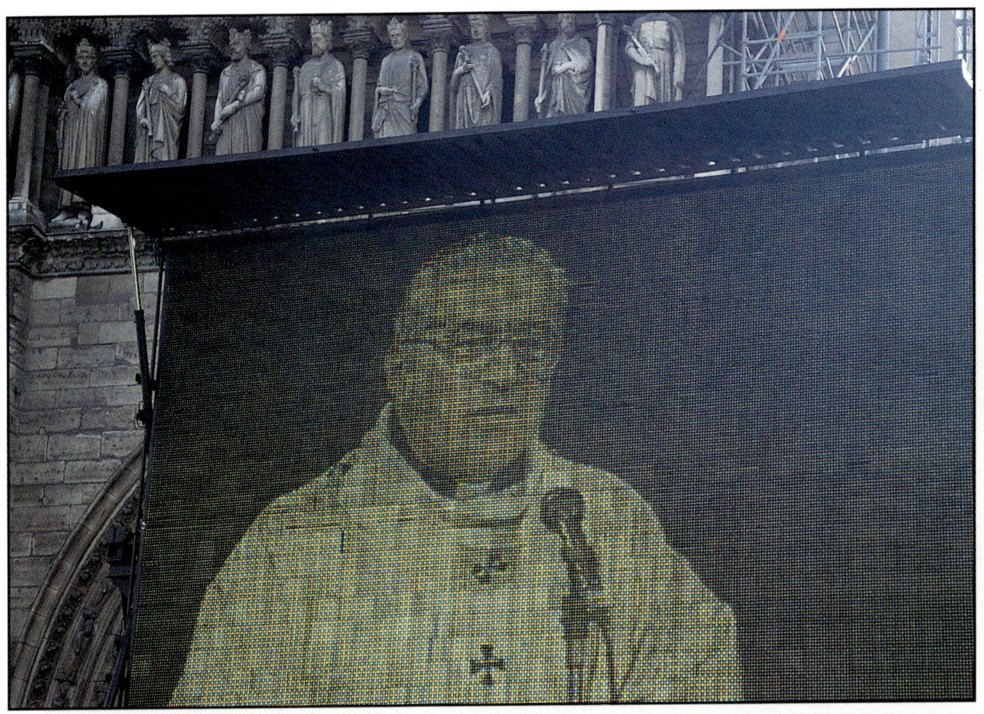

The Archeveque of Paris on the large TV screen outside Notre-Dame during Mass on May 7th.

Paris, lundi 8 mai

Paris, Monday, May 8th

I slept through the great parade along the *Champs Elysées* with the new president and the outgoing François Mitterand. Hey, I respect the fact that it's Victory in Europe Day, a national holiday! I got up and had lunch with my roommates Miriam and Claudia. Afterwards, we all went to *Parc Monceau* to relax in the sun, but everywhere we sat down was *pelouse interdite* (keep off the grass), so the guards chased us away. *Dommage* (too bad)! I then left the European ladies to look for that often-elusive great photo. The park itself was beautiful, *alors*, I took *pas mal de photos là* (quite a few photos there). Then I just walked and walked and walked, occasionally finding an interesting subject like a building covered with bougainvillea, a cool lamp post, torn billboards, people, dogs, rooftops, churches, avenues, monuments, statues, markets, food, and the list goes on.

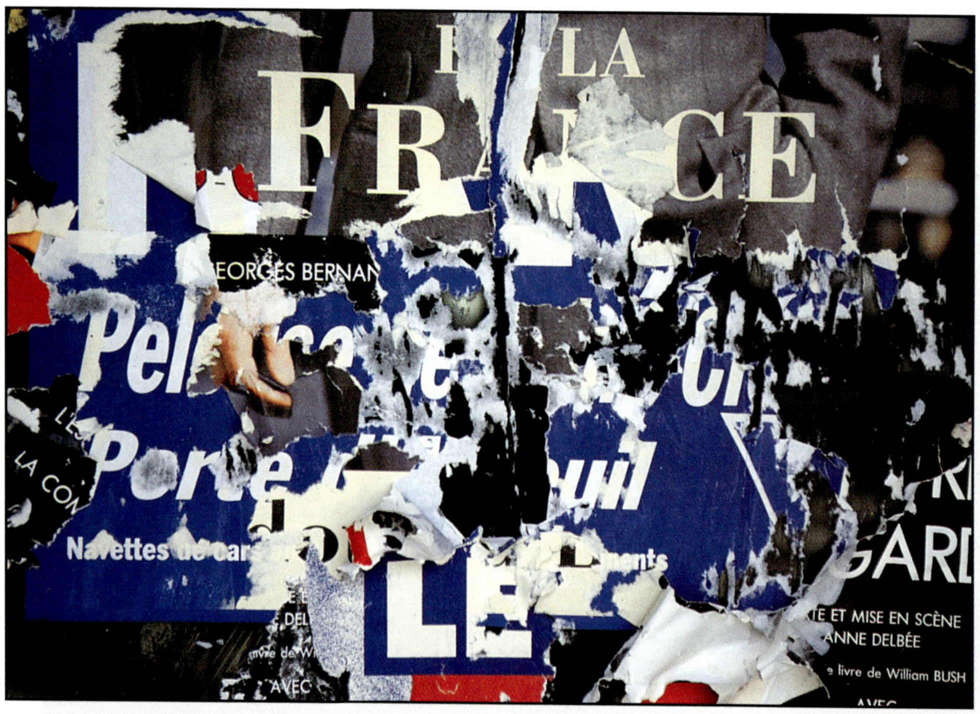

Ripped up billboards are a common sight in the City of Light, producing accidental art like this.

Most billboards in Paris are right at eye level. The layers of paper get stacked on top of older advertisements, and when, for some reason, the papers are ripped down, a very colorful, often beautiful accidental collage is the result. What I have to do is capture that image. It's really not as easy as it sounds. As with all photography, lighting is crucial for a crisp clear image, and with this particular kind of photography, composition is the art.

Overall, it was an uneventful day. I walked home and listened to my walkman and napped. We had *soupe de verdure* (vegetable purée soup) for an entrée, roast *pintade* (guinea) chicken for *le plat* (main course), and fresh fruit for *le déssert*. You might have the idea that the French eat scrumptious fattening sweets after every meal, but at home, fruit is the dessert of preference. Besides, the desserts you see in storefront windows are made by professionals, and *ça coûte cher* (they are expensive). However, when dining out, I have noticed that they usually have a sweet to complement *le repas* (the meal). Then I went to see a movie called *Elisa*. I went because Gérard Depardieu was in it; to my disappointment, he was only in the last half of the flick, but that part was good. *Moyen comme film* (average movie)!

Paris, mardi 9 mai

Paris, Tuesday, May 9th

This is the first ever European Economic Community Day, or EEC Day. It is not a holiday, thank God. It just seems like every Monday in May is *un jour férié* (a public holiday), and when you're only in school through May and paying *cher* (dearly) for language classes, you want to attend as many classes as possible, *non*?

I got up and had my usual hot tea with milk and sugar cubes. Then I caught a cab to the large *Printemps* department store to photograph the weekly ten o'clock fashion show. With my SB-24 flash and 400 ASA Fuji-chrome film, I took a load of pictures, especially of one stunning black woman. I took the *métro* back to the grand apartment, but before punching the code and going up, I bought a *croque monsieur* sandwich, an apricot tart, and an Orangina. It was delicious! Class was next. Then I went to *Prisunic* for some detergent, batteries, and Kleenex.

After a short rest, I went to a café and had *thé au lait* (tea with milk), while I wrote some *cartes postales* (postcards). At seven, Gilbert fixed me a plate of food, and I ate and ran to go hear the Isaac Stern concert. He played Mozart, Bartok, and Beethoven. I learned two things about concerts in Paris: the concert doesn't start until thirty minutes after the stated time on the ticket, and always ask if the seat is a *strapontin* (fold out), or you might be uncomfortable, like I was, the entire concert. But the music was excellent, and at least I was sitting quite close to the musicians.

The *Champs Elysées* was teeming with tourists as I maneuvered my way to *rue Arsène Houssaye* then down *avenue Bertie Albrecht*, across and down *avenue Hoche* and up *rue du Faubourg Saint-Honoré* to #225. Today I called Anny, my first French teacher in France, and she and Jean-Luc have invited me to visit Saint-Pont near Vichy. A *demain*! (See you tomorrow!)

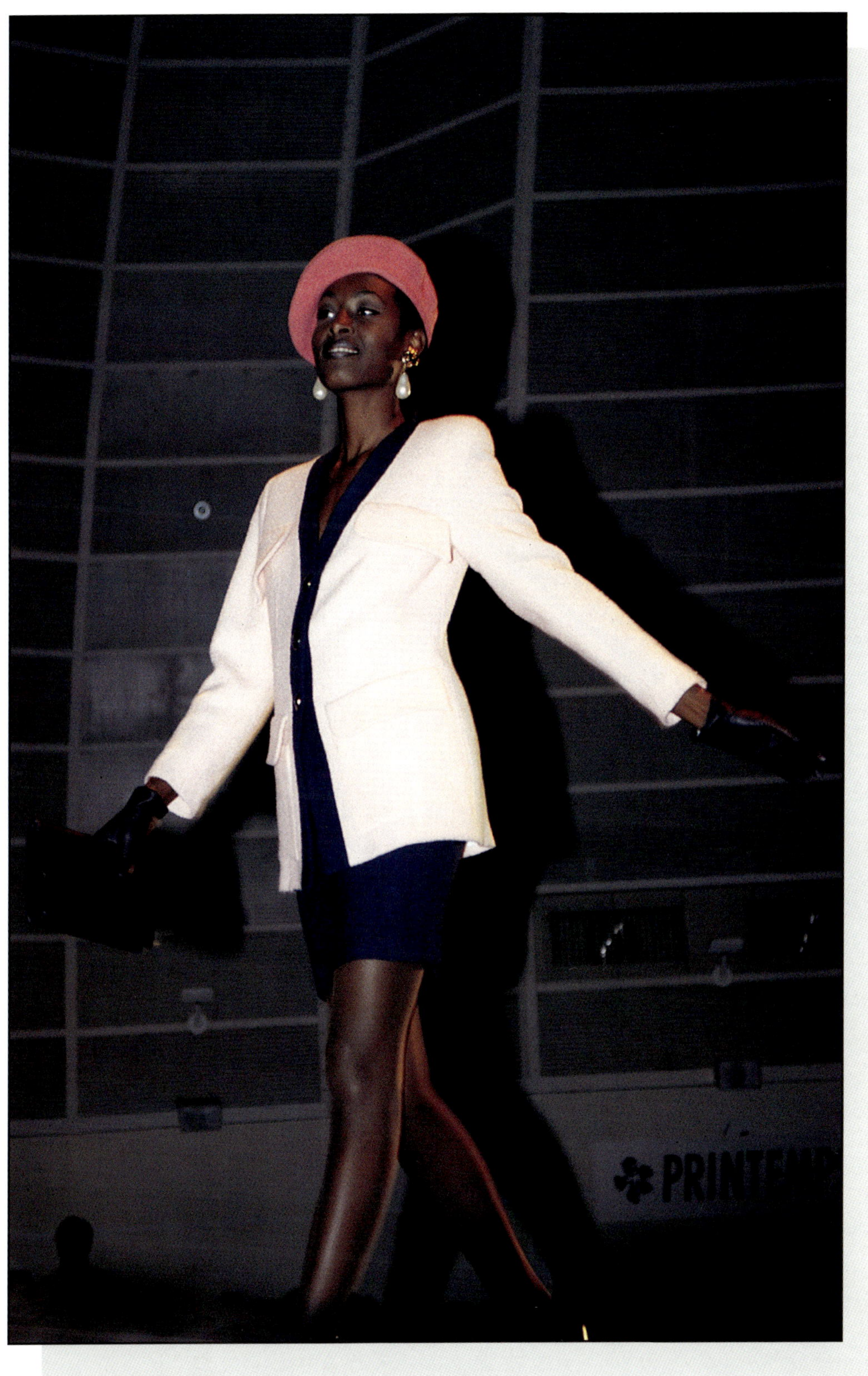

One of the weekly fashion shows at the Printemps department store on Boulevard Haussmann.

Paris, mercredi 10 mai

Paris, Wednesday, May 10th

Jerome was expecting my call, and by 10h30 the taxi dropped me off at 9, *rue Chevert*. He had done a lot of work this year, because the paintings were all over his apartment, like my photos back in Wilmington. He uses a lot of color, lots of symbols, and curiously, he also uses black markers to draw designs on the dry paint. Usually there are faces, very abstract though, and animals. Chagall comes to mind for me. His first exhibit for the year will be this Friday in a suburb of the capital. I offered my friend a *café*, and he insisted that we take our coffee there. *Un bon café*!

At 11h55 I caught a taxi to L'*Institute de Langue Française* for my daily lessons. My second course that day was an excellent literature class. Chrystelle, the *prof*, and I were the only ones there, so I had a private lesson on *Surréalisme*. I learned a great deal in our concentrated study of Appollinaire, Verlaine, and others.

After class, I changed some traveler's checks and remembered to go to *Le Texan* to watch the NBA playoffs. Unfortunately, the Bulls were not on, so I proceeded to have a few *Américanos* and talk with Al, the bar man. He had been in Paris for two years and really didn't care too much for the people or the language. He was English, but of Norwegian descent. A pessimist, it would seem! Derrick, an American who married a French girl so he could live and work here, just got a job at *Le Texan*. At this time, he was in the middle of a divorce, complete with French lawyers and courts.

I walked back around supper time and liver was served, but not for me. My hosts gave me a steak instead, and I was grateful. We had mashed potatoes with mashed carrots mixed together, and I'm definitely going to make this dish when I get home to the States. Simple and delicious! Later I did some homework and got into a conversation about Reims and Champagne with Claudia. She's in the Swiss School here, and we have great *discutions ensemble* (talks together). Tomorrow's a new day!

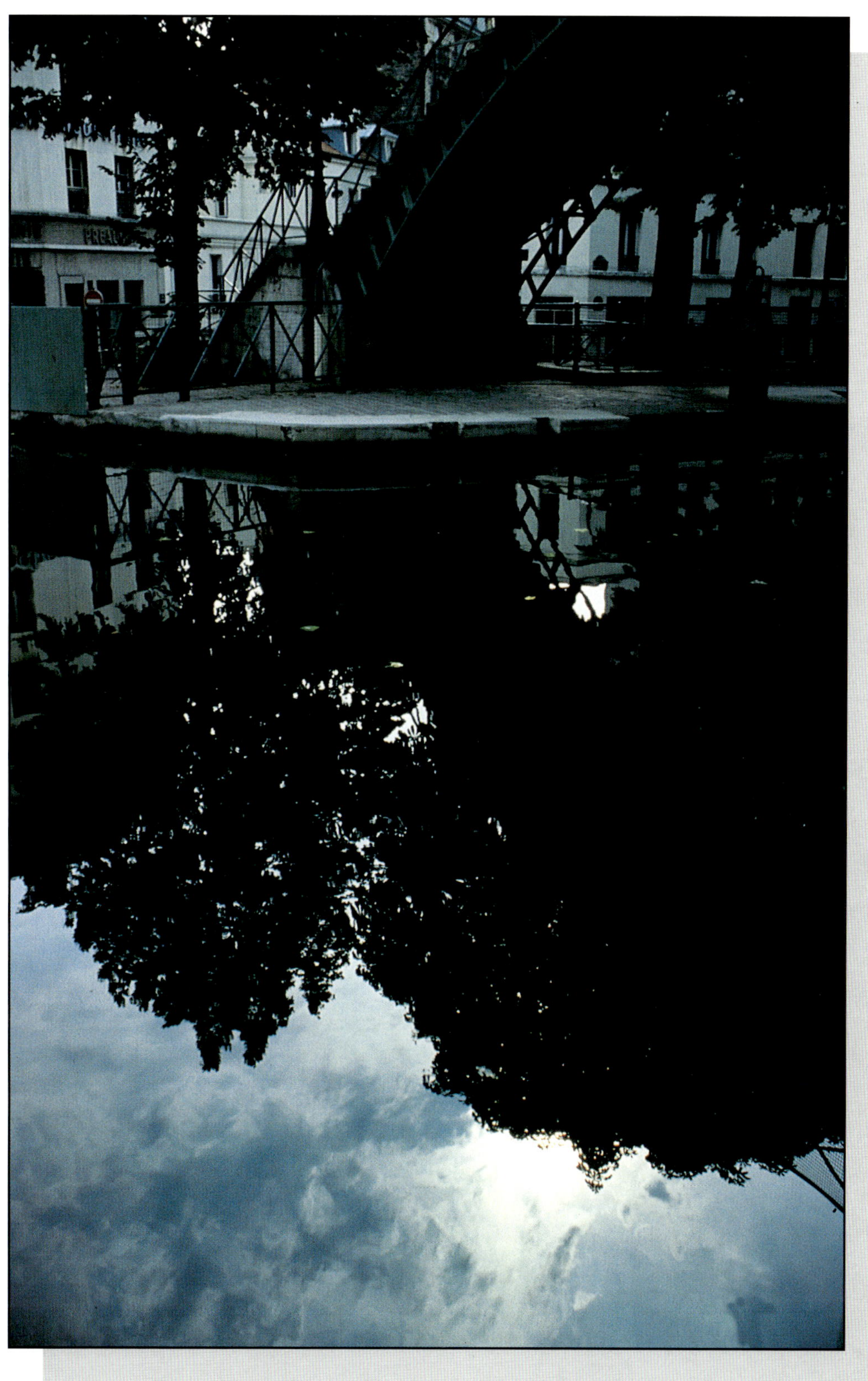

An eerie reflection at a walking bridge on the Canal Saint-Martin.

Paris, jeudi 11 mai

Paris, Thursday, May 11th

The French call it "*faire des courses.*" I began "making the rounds," or simply shopping, by going to *La* FNAC (a department store that sells quality photographic equipment, CDs and other kinds of music, books, and tickets to all kinds of concerts and art exhibits in the city), to get a polarizing filter and lens cleaner for my F4. I mailed some *cartes postales* at 4F30 each. *Tout est plus cher en France* (everything is more expensive in France)!

Alors, I had lunch at the *Bistro Romain* on the *Champs Elysées—salade frisée avec bacon fumé* (crispy salad with smoked bacon), *gigot d'agneau* (leg of lamb), *pomme frites* (French fries), and *cocktail de fruits éxotiques* (exotic fruit cocktail). *Excellente*! I walked around for a while, went by school to get a book, and took a glorious nap. It seems to me that when I live in a *grand ville* I need at least a short nap *chaque après-midi* (every afternoon). Maybe *la bonne cuisine* (the good food) makes me sleepy. After dinner, Gilbert and I made bananas *flambées* with Martinique rum. What a taste treat!

Then we had a stimulating conversation in the dining room with Michel, Thierry, Gilbert, Claudia, *et moi*. We talked about Greece, Turkey, Northern European women, false marrige contracts, and Gérard Depardieu in the film *Green Card*. I'm always thinking in French, even when writing in English. It's weird!

Devoirs et puis au lit (homework and then to bed). But before I hit the sack I want to mention that Guy and Catherine have invited me to visit her parent's country estate this weekend. I'm sure it will be fun—no trains, no subways, and no pollution!

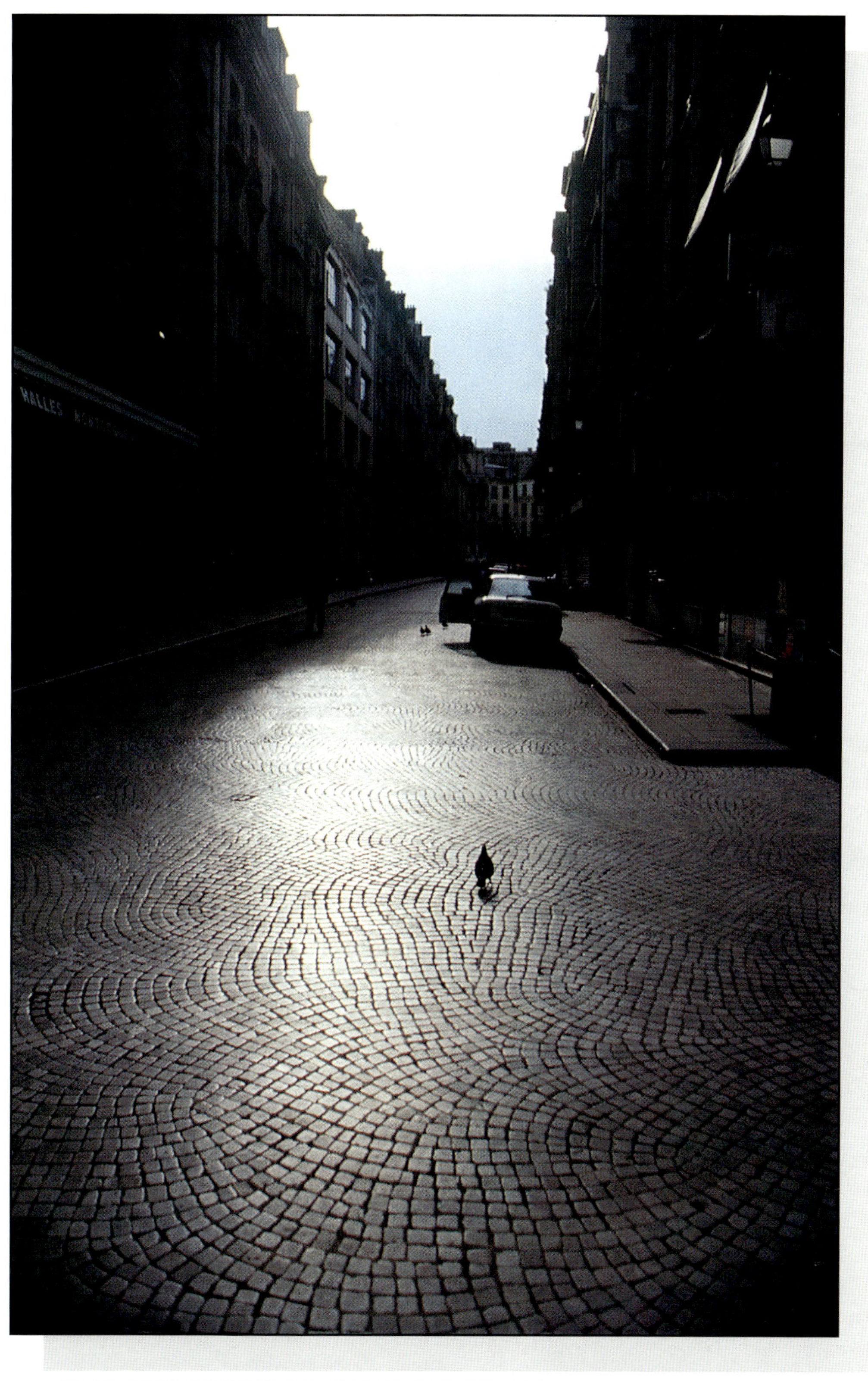

Light from above reflects down upon the patterned pavers of an almost deserted street.

Paris, vendredi 12 mai

Paris, Friday, May 12th

Slept late and went back to *La Poste* to ask about prices for sending packages airmail to the U.S. It was cheaper to send two 2-kilo boxes than one 4-kilo box. That 2-kilo limit irks the heck out of me! And if you just have to send a 2-kilo 100-gram box then you'll pay almost double. *C'est fou* (it's crazy)! However, if you are sending books and brochures or magazines you have the right to send up to five kilos at *un prix économique* (an economic price). Too bad chocolate and music don't fit into that category. *Attention*! They open boxes that say *livres, brochures, magazines,* and if they find something else inside, you'll never see your "books, brochures, and magazines" again. *Et oui, c'est la vie* (That's life)!

I walked back through the local outdoor market catching the scent of the seafood, then the fruit, and finally the wonderful fragrance of *viennoiserie* like *croissants, brioche,* and *tarte aux fruits.* We miss that kind of experience in the United States. It was almost noon, so I went to class. Four hours later I decided to go jogging, the red-blooded American that I am. I jogged through *Parc Monceau* and once around and everything was just dandy until right in front of the building I live in. There, my right calf muscle pulled, and I was limping again. Oh well!

For dinner we had cauliflower *au gratin,* poached eggs and ham in gelatin, fish sticks, and Claudia's *bordeaux.* After dinner we all went to the Leffe *brasserie* and drank delicious Belgian beer, while waiting for our *film* to start. We were going to see *The Last Seduction* in English with French *soutitres* (subtitles). All but French-made films are VO, for *version originale,* and French films are VF on the *Champs Elysées* and in many *cinemas* in Paris. At the *brass* we met some Canadian military guys who looked like linebackers from the NFL. They dug the girls, but we had to go. *Tant pis* (too bad)! *Bizzare comme film* (A very bizzare movie). Rain!

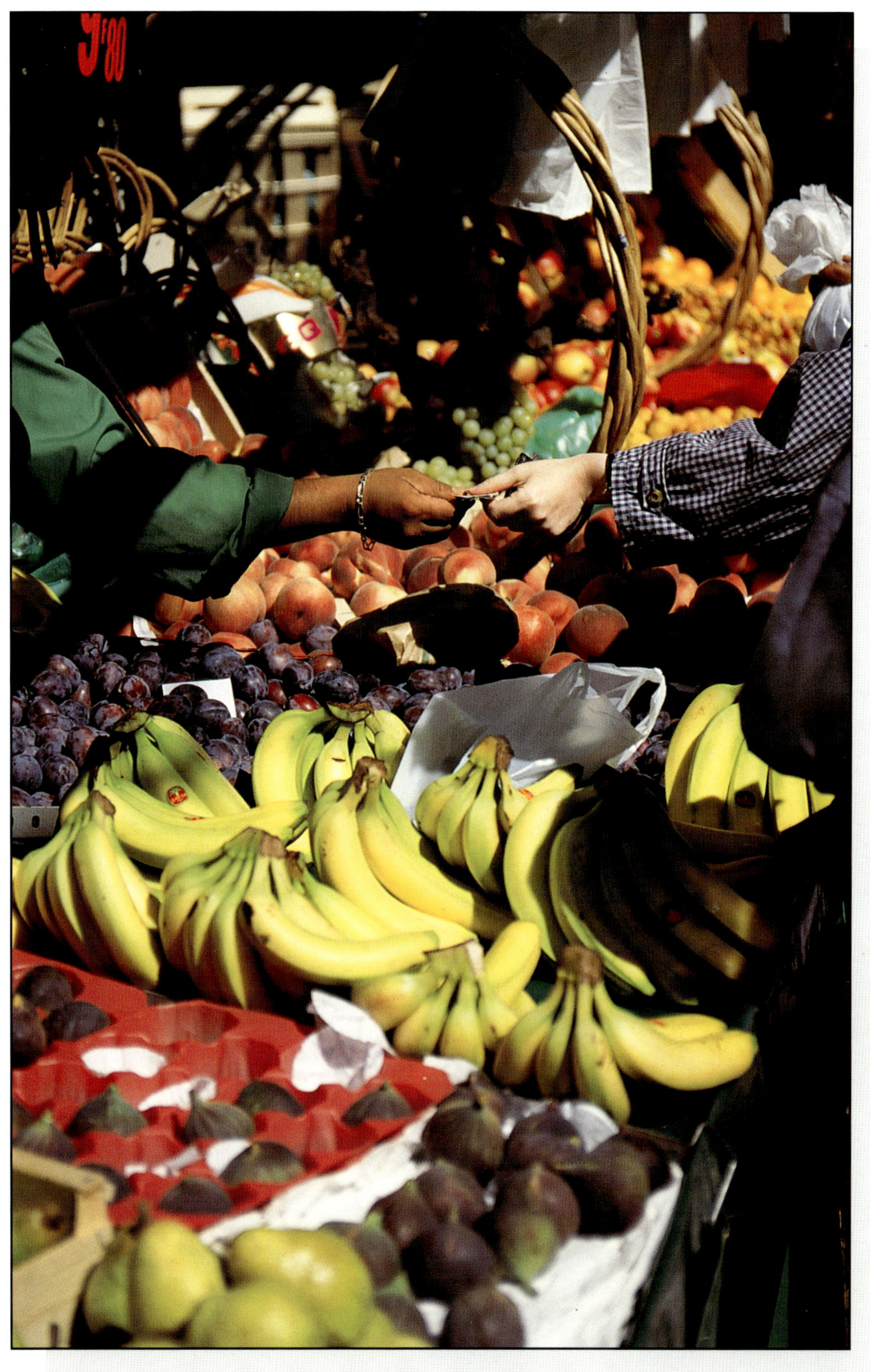

The outdoor market near Place des Ternes.

Vergers, samedi 13 mai

Vergers, Saturday, May 13th

Rain *encore*!

Up early, *petit déjeuner* (breakfast), and a wonderful café across from 22, *avenue de l'Opéra*. The coffee was 100% arabica and had the distinct taste of chocolate. *Très bon*! I walked over to #22 and punched *le code*, but once inside I had no idea where I was going. *Heureusement* (fortunately), the nice *concierge* lady knew my friends and told me where to go. They were all ready, so Guy and I went to get his car from the nearby garage at *Place Vendome*, and on the way he showed me some of the gorgeous jewelry that Catherine had designed for Van Cleef et Arpels and Boucheron—I was quite impressed. *Ça va de soit* (that goes without saying)! We drove back and got Catherine and headed out of Paris to the A6 autoroute towards Vergers, *dans la direction d'Orléans* (in the direction of Orléans).

La pluie (rain)! *Merde*!

But I was in France, so it was all right. The house and its surrounding grounds were so cool. Much of the construction was from the *moyen âge* (middle ages), like the huge stone fireplace, yet some of it was new, like the indoor/outdoor grill or *barbe à queue* (barbecue—yes, it is a French word, or at least it comes from France—the marriage of the words *barbe* [beard] and *queue* [tail], which is how they roast a pig, from its head to its tail).

The property was sixteen acres of lush green—everything that grows, along with streams, gardens, and guest houses. There was an ultra-modern kitchen with brilliant, rust-colored marble everywhere. Monsieur Mathon has designed precious jewelry for many years, and he explained to me how he got into the business. I'll guard his secret for now. He has worked for Crystolfle and Boucheron. *Alors*, the house was like a mountain house in North Carolina—stone everywhere, with wood inside, and the wonderful scent of burning wood all around.

Lunch was incredible—*muscat de Cap Corse* for *l'apéro*; *Côtes du Rhône*; some kind of meat *terrine* of pork and entrails; tomatoes, fresh basil, mozzarella covered in a vinaigrette; tremendous tuna steaks wrapped in mountain laurel leaves, seasoned with salt and pepper for six hours, then grilled to perfection and eaten with reverent delight; *un plateau de fromages* (a plate of cheese), *encore du vin* (more wine), succulent and sweet pear tart, *café*, and *des bonbons*. *Quel bon repas* (What a great meal)!

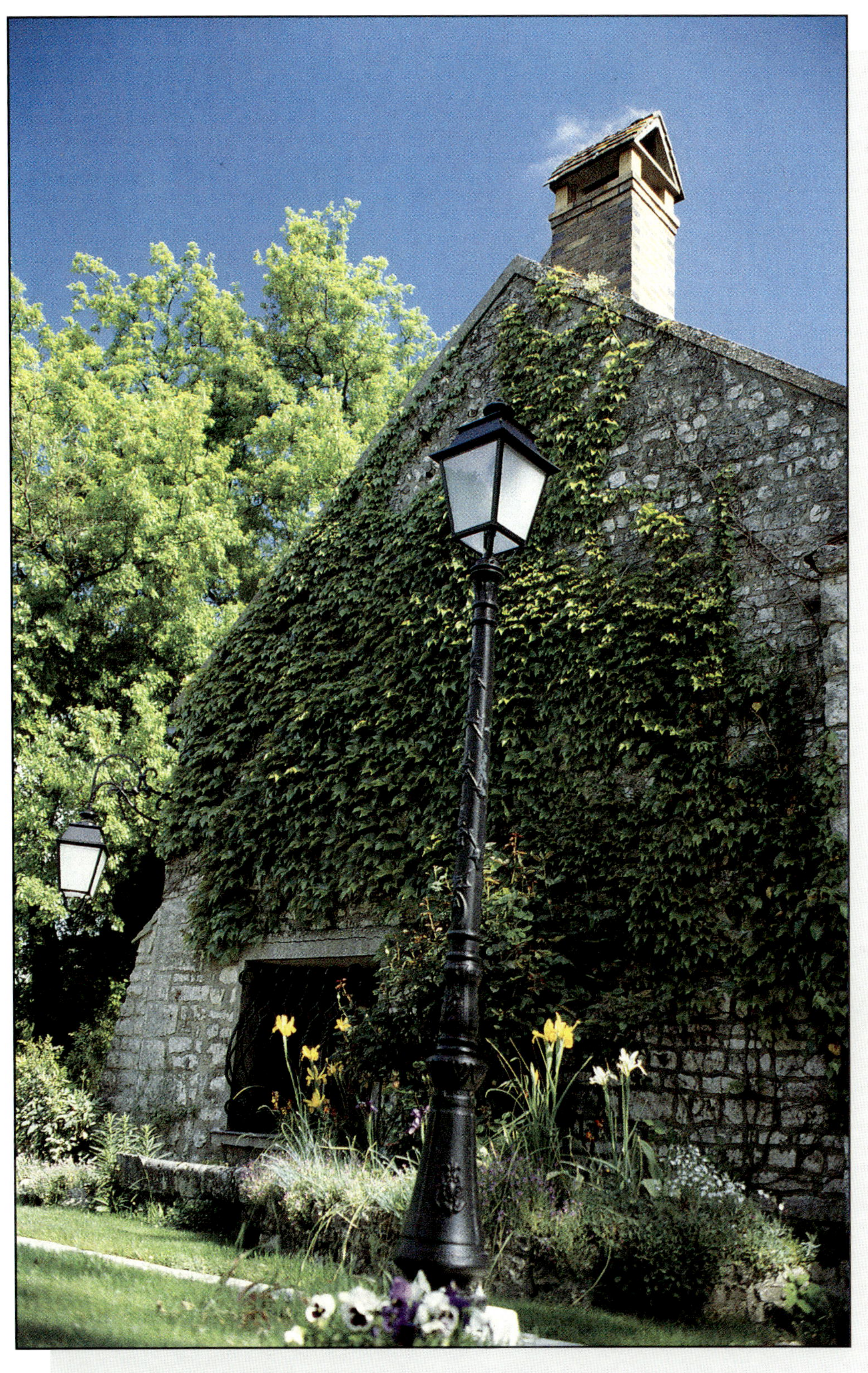

The entrance to the Mathons' country estate.

Later we explored the nearby village of Chateau Landon, with no rain, but lots of clouds—clean and refreshing, though. My camera got some use, but I think it was too gray for pretty pictures. I bought a cheap cigar and a *carte téléphonique* (calling card) that said "Call Home" on it. We were tired so we walked back to take *du repos* (naps) at the estate. Dinner was excellent! We had rare roast beef, roasted potatoes, foot-long white and purple asparagus with a delicious vinaigrette, a dish you eat with your hands, *un plateau de fromages*, and fruit cocktail.

After dinner we sat by the fire, and I played with the little one I called *le mouton gris* (the gray sheep), which was really a fifteen-year-old poodle. A*u lit*! B*onne nuit*! B*ons rêves*! D*ors bien*! A *demain*! (To bed! Good night! [procounced "Bun nwee"] Sweet dreams! Sleep well! See you tomorrow!)

Vergers, dimanche 14 mai

Vergers, Sunday, May 14th

We all got up and had a delicious *petit déjeuner* of *brioche, croissants*, jams and jellies, fresh-squeezed orange juice, and coffee. The weather was cool and clear, and we drove to a nearby village for a kind of giant outdoor garage sale called a *brocante*. These days, the French do not sell most of the valuable objects from days of old in their attics and cellars, so treasure hunting can be a lesson in futility, according to Guy. Monsieur Mathon sped us home in his *grosse citroën*, where we prepared for another meal. For lunch we began, *comme d'habitude* (as usual), with *un aperitif* called a Kir, which is simply dry white wine and *crème de cassis*, a black currant liqueur normally made in Dijon. We enjoyed *langoustines* (Dublin Bay prawns) with homemade *mayonnaise*, rare leg of lamb, beautiful oblong red radishes with butter and a special gray sea salt, green beans in garlic sauce, white beans with carrots and onions, all kinds of delectable cheeses (the odor of which could make you faint), fruit salad sweetened with real cane syrup, and coffee. Another *repas incroyable* (incredible meal)! And I left out all the white and red wine we drank. By that time it was 15h30, so some of us napped for a while.

At 18h00 we trudged through the muddy yard to a tiny plastic boat at the edge of a stream and, crazy as it sounds, four of us got in for a ride. Our shoes covered in thick mud, my expensive camera in hand, *alors*, Monsieur Mathon decided to paddle the tub standing up. Several times we almost flipped into the cold French waters before Catherine got out on the bank—saved! My camera was safe too, and Catherine took a picture of us in the boat. We continued on with my "total enjoyment" until we were finally back at shore. Funny thing is, I think Monsieur Mathon thought that I was a little seasick. I just didn't want to be rude and say take me back, even at the expense of my "traveling companion." After the shakedown cruise, we prepared *encore une fois* (again) for a dinner. They all ate *boudin noir*, which is black blood sausage, but I just don't eat that stuff. I was lucky enough to eat the leftovers from previous meals—asparagus you eat with your hands, roast beef, green salad, fruit salad, and a pear tart. Wow, did we eat and drink this weekend!

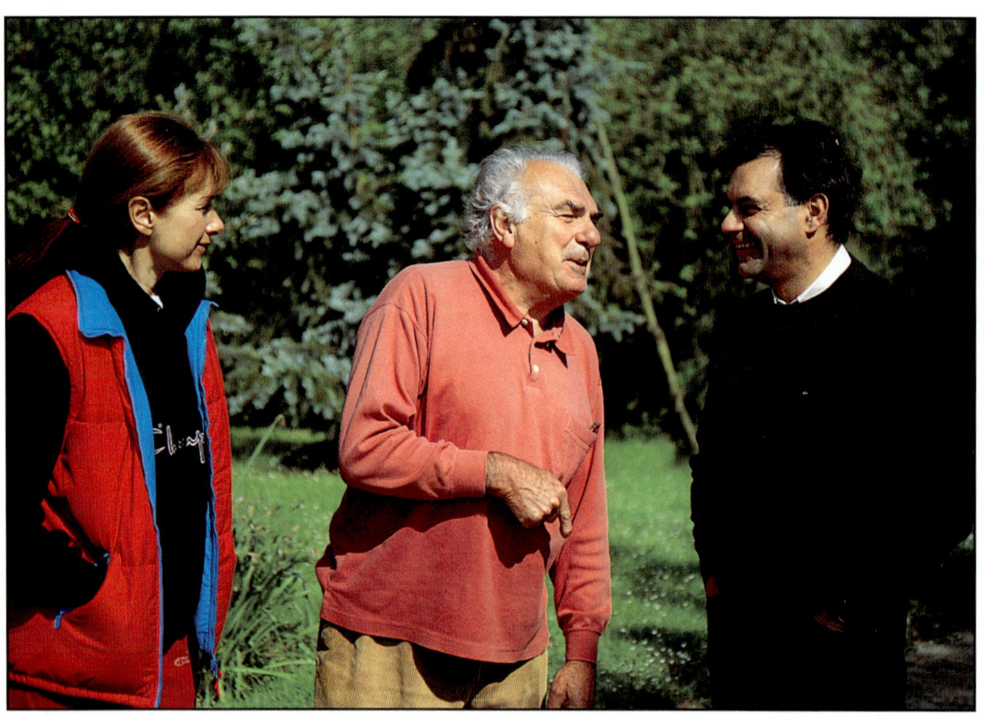

Catherine, Monsieur Mathon, and Guy.

Paris, lundi 15 mai

Paris, Monday, May 15th

I woke up in a funk, maybe from the weekend, and I just had to have one of those French *café espressos* and a warm *croissant* with strawberry jam. That did it! That put me back in a positive frame of mind. Then I went to class and really enjoyed learning tons of new vocabulary. The ILF is a good language school, but to wear out an old cliché, you only get out of it what you put in. After *le cours* (the class) I caught the *métro* to *Les Halles* to have tea with milk and a *tarte tatin* (upside-down caramelized apple pie), at the famous Au Père Tranquille. I sat inside because there was hardly a table available on the terrace, *en plus* (even more), everybody looked so cool in their black leather jackets and hard-soled shoes that I felt a little out of place with my tennis shoes and Carolina sweat shirt. As is common in front of popular cafés in Paris, a clown entertained us by making fun of passersby. A crowd gathered, and several dogs showed up like magic. He used them in his little skit as if he had rehearsed for days and days, and yet you were never sure if the dogs were his, because they seemed to come out of nowhere.

I decided to make the long walk home, so I went by the church of *Saint-Eustache*, bore left, went around the *Palais Royal*, found the *rue de Rivoli*, took a right after the Louvre at *Place des Pyramides*, worked my way up the *rue Saint-Honoré en faisant leche vitrine* (a phrase which literally means "licking store windows"), to the *rue du Faubourg Saint-Honoré*, and was home. Before punching *le code* and going up, I went into a nearby *pharmacie* to buy good *shampooing, aspirine* (you can only buy it in French drugstores), and Dermophil Indien lip balm. By the way, take an ample supply of your favorite aspirin with you to France, because the French are still in the Dark Ages as far as that is concerned. All they have are horse pills and sour chewables. No big deal! Just an observation—OK, a complaint.

For dinner we had a salad of mixed greens and tomatoes, creamy *blanquette de veau* (veal) with lots of fresh *champignons* (mushrooms), cheeses, and fruit. I decided I would have to learn how to make that veal dish with cream and mushrooms, because it is simply wonderful. After the copious meal, we watched French television, which is very challenging to understand. When people use a lot of slang and *mangent les mots* (eat words), I really have a hard time understanding. I guess it's the same for all languages. I'm sure I eat words and

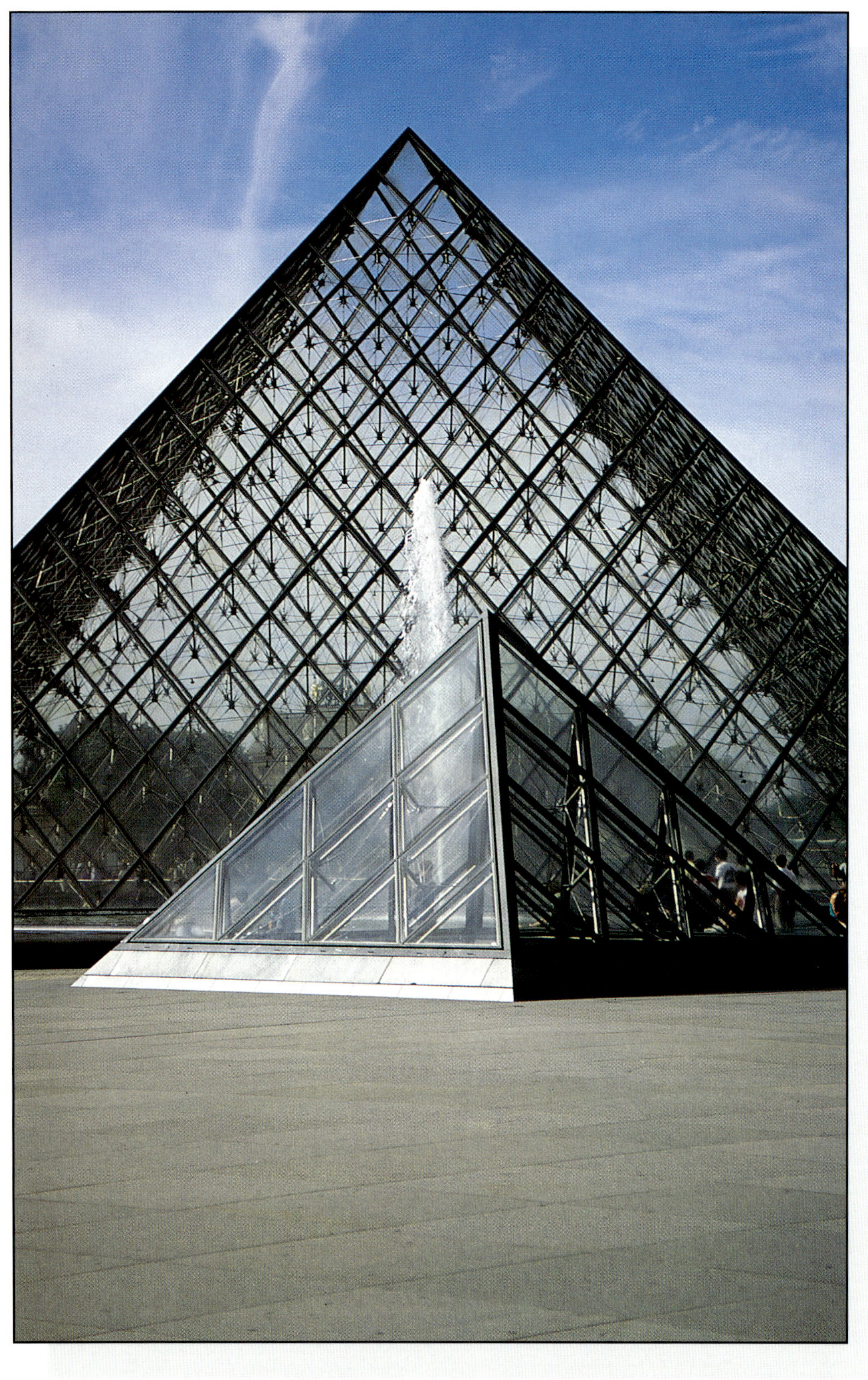

*The controversial Pyramid
designed by I. M. Pei at the entrance to the Louvre.*

use slang, but I'm just not aware of it. As a world traveler, I have learned to speak English slowly and clearly to foreigners as a measure of consideration for them and for myself. French people, however, take such pride in their native tongue that to slow down their speech would be blasphemy to their religion. *Dors bien* (Sleep well)!

Paris, mardi 16 mai

Paris, Tuesday, May 16th

Paris is one city that shines from within when it is raining. *Malgré* (despite) the weather, there are always worthwhile things to see and do if your day doesn't find you behind a desk. I went to class, which was very interesting, because everybody had a chance to *parler beaucoup* (speak a lot). *Alors, après la classe* (after class) I went home to study and listen to French radio. It's funny that now France has some privately owned radio stations that play whatever they like, while the state-owned ones are required to air a certain *pourcentage* of French programming and music. English-speaking Top 40 music dominates private stations, so I always listen to the predominantly French music stations, because it helps me learn new words and expressions as well as the proper pronunciation, which means everything to French ears. Besides, there are some excellent French tunes by singers like Françis Cabrel, Alain Suchon, and Axelle Red. In America we are not even aware of the *tubes* (hits) from this creative nation. It is

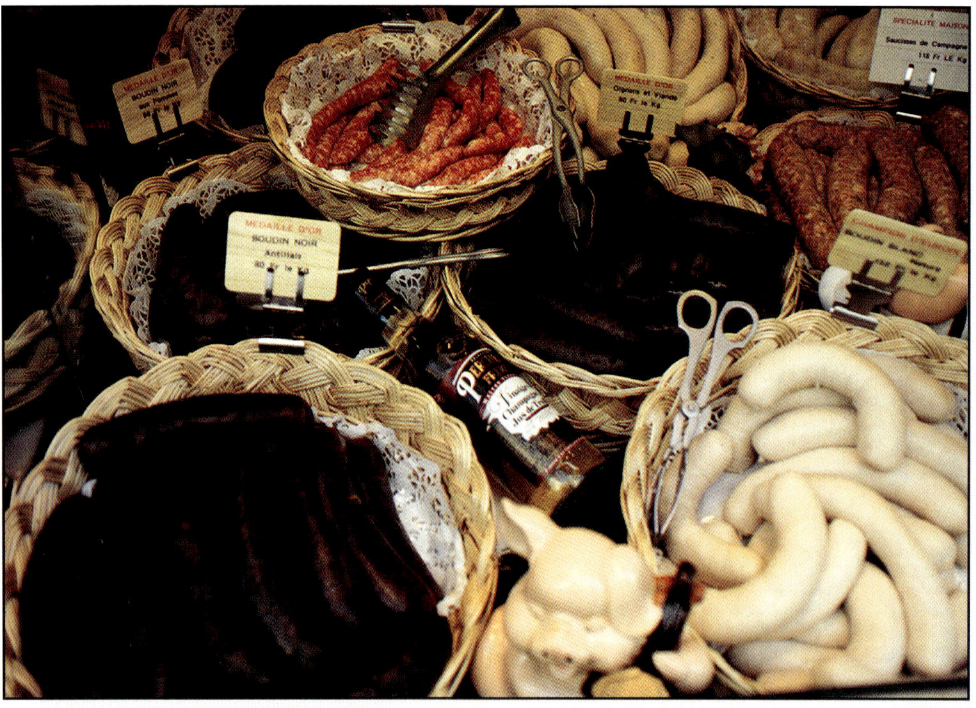

Black boudin blood sausage, white boudin, and other pork sausages.

truly a shame, because understanding lyrics is definitely not a prerequisite to enjoying good music *point à la ligne* (period).

Dinner was early for me since I was going to a piano recital at the Pleyel music hall across the street at 18h30. What a delicious meal! Big, succulent Toulousian sausage, *tous petits* lentils with carrots, onions, and bacon, apple *compote,* and a George Killian's. The French have all sorts of the moist raw kinds of sausage and also the dry stick kinds that are perfect for picnics, because no cooking is required. With all the pork we have in North Carolina, you'd think that we would have more than two or three kinds of sausage. But there are two reasons why I shouldn't complain. One is because it's just one more reason to go to France, and two is that maybe folks back home are so content with what they have that change would mean war. I don't know. The French have been making sausage now for over a thousand years, *alors,* maybe in 2800 we'll be making that many varieties of sausage. I'm complaining. I hate that, but . . . no complaining!

The music tonight was beautiful, and the actor that accompanied the *pianiste* was brilliant. I've never seen or heard anything like it. The actor announced names of skits and narrated each one while the woman played a different piece of music for each. I loved it. A *demain*!

Paris, mercredi 17 mai

Paris, Wednesday, May 17th

I had my usual continental breakfast, and caught a taxi to *Place Saint-Michel*, where the weather looked like it was going to clear up for an instant. That's all it was, *un instant*. So I just walked around and licked a few store windows and ended up at *Le Cour Rohan*, a neat little *salon de thé* near *Le Procope*. *Malheureusement* (unfortunately), *le restaurant étais fermé jusqu'à midi* (the restuarant was closed until noon). Oh well! I stopped at a café and had an endive and Swiss cheese salad and a Coke, leaving just enough room in my belly for some kind of goody, most likely from *une patisserie*. *Et oui*! The fresh pear tart with a crunchy crust was just the the thing *le medecin a commandé* (the doctor ordered). Unreal!

I found a cab and went to class. We were still learning about *La Cause*, which is *très difficile* (very difficult). After a stimulating four hours, I got my camera and went directly to the Eiffel Tower to shoot. Unfortunately, the top was closed due to forty-knot winds. I did make it to the second floor though, and took some shots of the green gardens below. The wind was blowing me all around, disturbing my photography, so I descended with a crowd of tourists to see what looked good from below. When I was leaving I took several wide angle shots from beneath the enormous yet graceful structure, and they could be intriguing. Once again, I chose to make a long walk home, because lots of daylight remained, and Paris has to be the most beautiful city to walk through in the whole world. First I passed the *métro* stops of Trocadero, then Boissonière, then Kléber, and finally Etoile, and I was practically home, so I decided to enjoy a few *Américanos* while I addressed some *cartes postales* in a café of no renown.

At the Marchand's we had a delicious meal of roast leg of lamb; roasted potatoes; carrots; string beans; wonderful, creamy, two-inch-thick *quiche à la Gilbert*; *fromage blanc "du terroir"* (white creamy cheese from country farmers), and strawberries to go with it. Oh, and wine, *bien sûr* (of course). Yes, I was gaining weight, but no, I would not continue to eat like this. No way! *Désormais, je suis au regime* (From now on, I'm on a diet). Right! "French diet" is an oxymoron.

Our conversation that evening was about how different nationalities handle living in Paris with a French family. Jeanne-Marie has had a lot of experience with students, and we decided that it usually depends on the individual, *même si* (even if) some folks don't seem to adjust well to French life. She told me of one

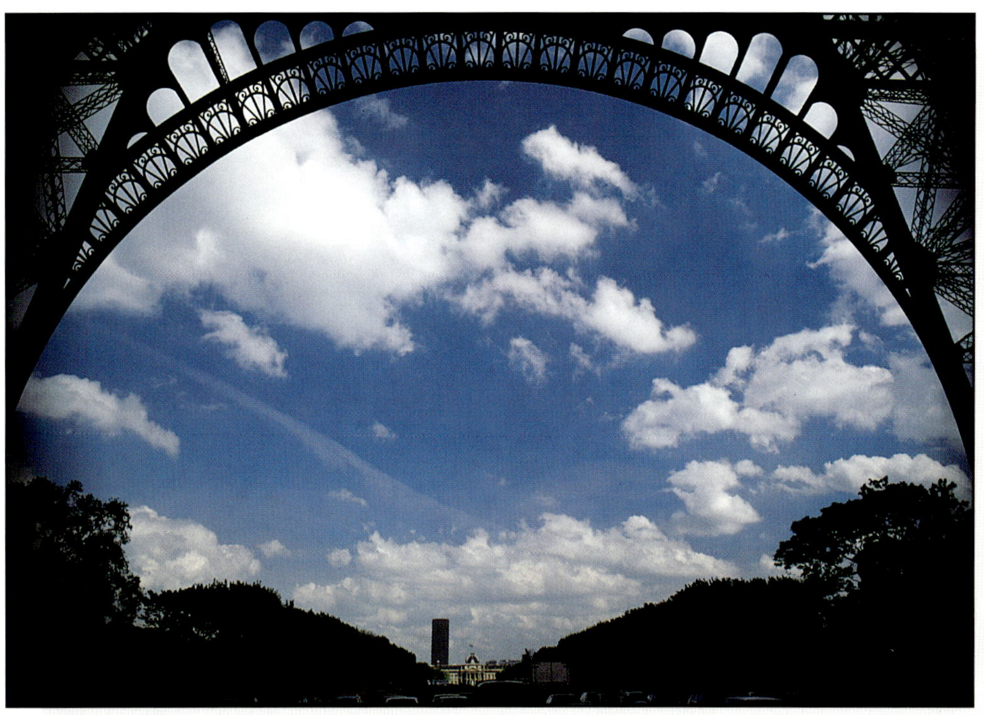

A view from under the Eiffel Tower, also controversial when it was first built.

twenty-year-old *Américaine* who literally wrote eighty postcards home in a matter of weeks. This gal hardly ever left her room except to go to class. Apparently, every day she would receive about four letters from home, which she would savor for hours in her room. I cannot judge this behavior, but it would be considered *une tragedie* by most.

I left out the satisfying smoke I enjoyed, a Montecristo #4. B*onne nuit*!

Paris, jeudi 18 mai

Paris, Thursday, May 18th

La *pluie* (rain) again!

I'm tired of this rain—it falls more here than in London, if you can believe that. It put a damper on my work—in *noir et blanc* (black and white) the misty rain can create a beautiful surrealistic photograph, but I'm not shooting black and white.

I walked to an SNCF (*Societé Nationale des Chemins de Fer*) ticket office to buy *mon billet* (my ticket) to Nantes, *aller simple* (one way), because I would eventually drive back to Paris. My train leaves *La Gare Montparnasse* at 7h50 Saturday, the twenty-seventh of this month.

I marched through the rain back to the *grand apartment* to listen to the radio and relax before class. There are no other men in any of my classes, and being single, you'd think I would be in heaven. Not so! Maybe the Parisian women have lifted my standards a little too high. After *le cours* I began working my way to *Le Centre George Pompidou*, a museum that is built inside out, in the *quartier Beaubourg*. My first stop was at a McDonald's for a delicious double cheeseburger and a Coke with plenty of ice. Then a little while later I saw some *publicité* for a new men's cologne called "Niagara," and apparently it had not yet come out in the *parfumeries*—a lady informed me that it would be available before I left France. I like original colognes like Caroline Herrera and Opium, which hadn't yet come out in America at the time of this writing.

Without my "traveling companion" around my neck, I believe I missed three good photo opportunities. Hey, it happens! Finally, around 19h20, I arrived at the Centre and met my friend, Catherine, and her office group of about fifteen people. We had an excellent guide for the Brancusi sculpture and photography exhibit, and my one word for the show was "inspiring." He came to Paris from Romania in the late 1800s and attended L'*Ecole Des Beaux Arts*. Rodin, for whom Brancusi worked, was his mentor, and much of the earlier works show that influence. The entire lecture was in French, and it was a challenge to keep up with our fast-talking, erudite Frenchman who obviously loved speaking about art, Brancusi in particular. His works ranged from a long and beautiful metal fish to huge abstract sculptures in wood and in stone. He photographed his sculptures almost exclusively in *noir et blanc*, and became quite good at it.

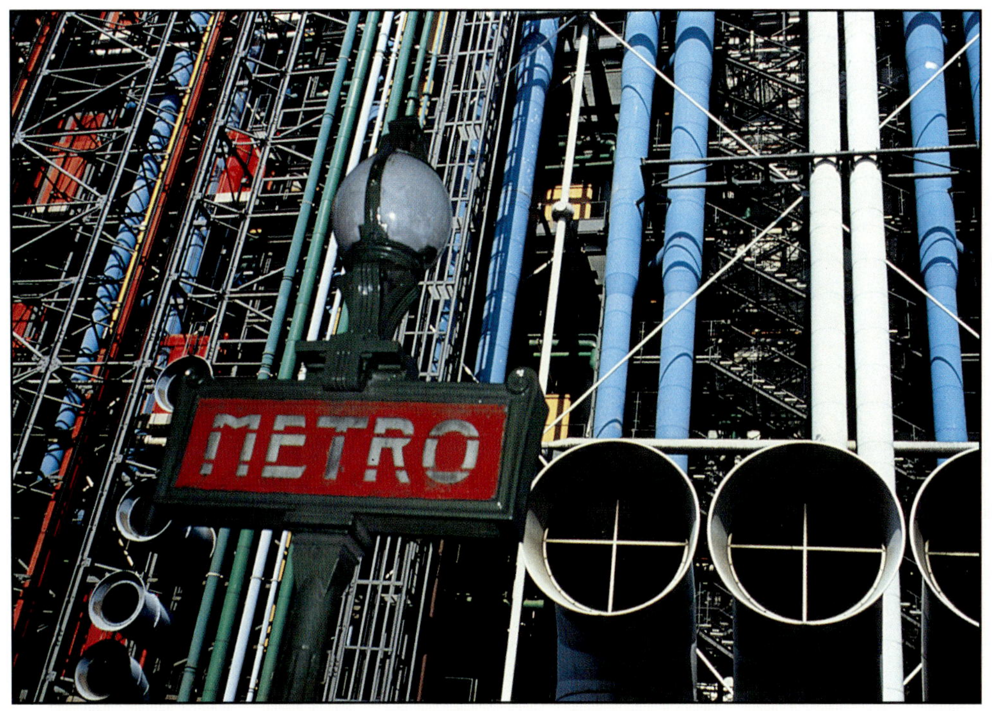

The Centre George Pompidou,
a building that was built inside out–controversial too.

Afterwards, six of us went to one of a chain of restaurants called *Léon de Bruxelles* and ate steamed mussels prepared in a variety of sauces with french fries. Since I am a "typical American" in France, I just had to put loads of ketchup on my fries. I drank *une grand biere* (a large beer) of 50 cl, and everybody else had wine. Some had dessert, but not me—I decided to torture myself. Catherine treated me to the copious and tasty meal, and we all parted, they *à pied* (on foot), while I went *en métro* (in the subway). *Merci et salut* Catherine!

Paris, vendredi 19 mai

Paris, Friday, May 19th

I got up and had my tea, toasted *baguette*, butter, and jam. Had my cup of liquid energy at Le Hoche and went to class. After class, I had a meal at a strange restaurant owned by some *Japonais*. What I ordered was supposed to be *Coquilles Saint-Jacques*, but it wasn't very creamy, and it had potatoes in it. It was good though, and dessert was simply sublime—chocolate mousse covered with chocolate fondant, a thin layer of hard caramel inside, sitting in a puddle of vanilla and chocolate *crème anglaise*. Wow—I was hungry; it was either eat there or have a filet of fish sandwich *chez* McDoe.

Since we had a lot of daylight left, I grabbed my camera and went walking towards *avenue* Matignon to see about buying one of HAIJIMA's awesome paintings. They are so cool—scenes of *les toits* (rooftops) *de* Paris in a kind of grayish haze with light almost passing through the canvas. The rooftops are discernible, but as you look below, things become much less defined. Some are of

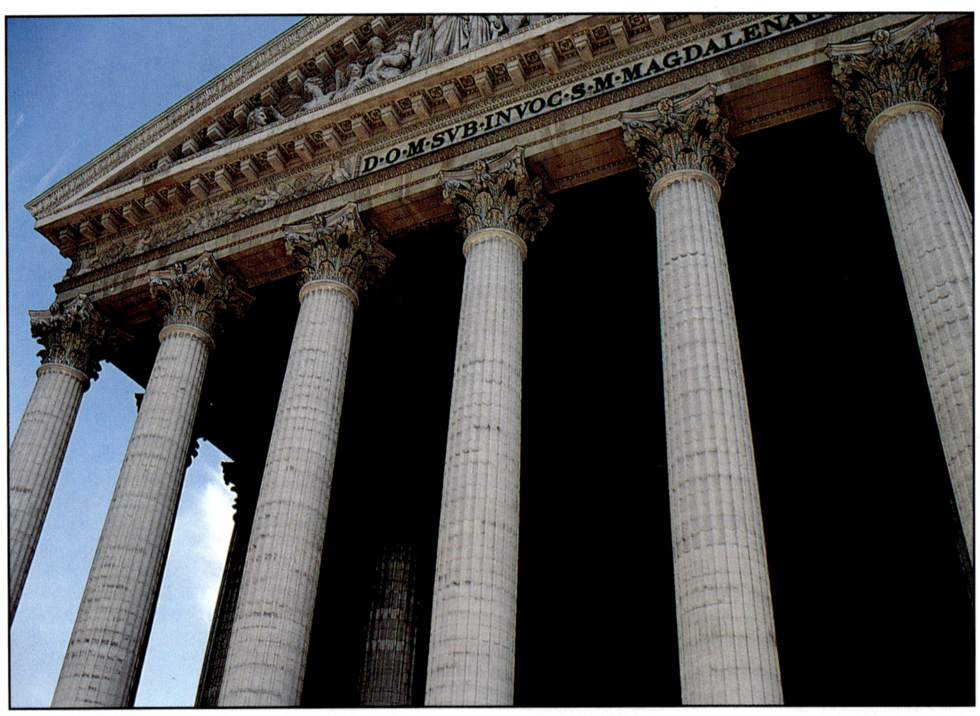

La Madeleine, a church that looks more like a monument.

recognizable buildings like *Notre-Dame*, while others are just *toits* as seen from his studio. I couldn't afford the large ones, and the small one that I wanted had already sold. *Pas de probleme* (No problem)! The gallery said it would call me if the painting I liked became available by chance. In the art world, "sold" only means sold when the money is in hand. I continued down the *rue du Faubourg Saint-Honoré* and took some shots here and there. I stopped near La Madeleine and walked on to *Le Palais Royal*, where I caught the *métro* back to Place des Ternes.

Dinner was short and light, luckily—trout in parchment paper, rice, and a salad. Even though I was not hungry, the trout had very little flavor, so here is my *recette* (recipe) for trout: one whole trout, olive oil, salt, pepper, herbs, and a little butter, all in parchment paper or even foil; bake at 350 degrees for fifteen to twenty minutes. *C'est facile*! (It's easy!)

Giverny, samedi 20 mai

Giverny, Saturday, May 20th

Wow—my natural alarm clock works! When I need to wake up in the mornings, I wake up at the right time or earlier without an alarm clock or anything. Today I wanted to get up at 7h00 and my instincts woke me at 6h45. Not bad, but I wonder if I could trust my built-in system after a late night of drinking in a *boite de nuit* (night club). Probably not!

I had my breakfast and then walked a couple of miles to La Gare Saint-Lazare, but to my dismay, there was no 9h15 train. There was an eight-something train, and I had just missed it. *Merde*! Next train: 12h30. *Alors*, I took the subway to République and just wandered my way back to *la gare* (the station). But the first thing I did was stop in a cool little *salon de thé* for coffee and a *financier*, a pound-cake-like treat made from almond extract and almond powder in the shape of a little gold boullion brick (maybe that's why they call it a *financier*). The best ones I ever had came from a wonderful *salon de thé* in Vichy called *Le Pourcin Bleu*, but those were round instead of rectangular. Ladurée, at 16, *rue Royale* near *La Madeleine*, has excellent *financiers* too, but theirs are pointed. I bet Fauchon makes good ones.

I had the opportunity to work *chez* Fauchon in the *laborotoire patissière* (pastry kitchen) for six weeks in the spring of 1984. My friend, Philippe, who is Chinese-Vietnamese, born in Madagascar and raised in Paris, worked with me, and we had a blast learning about all their delights. We were staying in his cousin's flat in the northern suburb of Saint-Ouen for free at the time, because his cousin was visiting a gal in Brittany. The matress on the floor made a nice bed, and the place was *propre* (tidy). We couldn't have asked for more. Everyday we would either drive my rental car or take the *métro* to Saint-Lazare, walk to Fauchon, and enter the world of skilled *patissiers* (pastry chefs). Phil had no problem with the language and jumped right in, making fruit tarts and *fruits déguisés*, which are burnt-sugar-coated almond paste, cherries, pineapple, and other fruits and nuts.

My first job was to roll *croissants* on the cold marble counter top. It ain't easy—your hands can warm up the butter in the *pâte* (dough) and make the *croissant* ribless when it is cooked, and thus below Fauchon standards. The roll has to be one quick motion either away or towards you without pressing too hard on the middle or on the sides. The slightest pinch with the thumb and index finger completes the task, *mais ce n'est pas évident* (but it's not obvious).

Our hours were 8h00 to 13h30, at which time we would follow the other culinary artists up to the cafeteria to enjoy a delicious feast that included all we wanted of the imperfect pastries from that morning. Believe me, we never had room for dessert. I feel like I have just "pulled a Proust" by remembering a pastry, with that memory evoking many other memories. Speaking of memories, just as I was on my way to catch the train I ran into my friend, Kelly Jones, whom I had not seen in ten years. *Petit monde* (Small world)! We took photos of each other, and I rushed to the station *pour attraper le train* (to catch the train). At Vernon I shared a cab to Giverny with a couple from Michigan. Monet's house, garden, and water garden were wonderful, even with the unavoidable crowd. Everything seems to be painted in blue and yellow *à la Monet*. Even the restaurant, Les Agapanthes, where I had lunch, was *bleu et jaune* (blue and yellow). I was in *Le Paradis*—those are my two favorite colors. Then it was back to Vernon, where I bought some parting gifts for Gilbert and Jeanne-Marie. I also bought some *fromage de brebis* (sheep cheese), some *chévre* (goat cheese), and some *cent pourcent* (100%) *arabica* coffee from Hawaii. What a country! If it's the best the world has to offer, count on it being available in France.

When I arrived home I washed up and changed and had *un verre de vin* (a glass of wine), with Jeanne-Marie and Diane, which led to another, and so I called Flo to tell them I would be late for dinner. After *un verre de vin*, I called Flo to change my *reservation* to the next evening. The three of us ended up dining at Le Verre en Bouteille on avenue des Ternes. We all had *salades niçoises* with fresh tuna, and I had dessert—cherry *crème brulée*. What a civilized country! We spoke too much English though. When in France, *je préfère parler français* (I prefer to speak French). Diane loves New York and plans to retire there one day, and I love Paris and plan to live there one day. *Salut*! A *demain*!

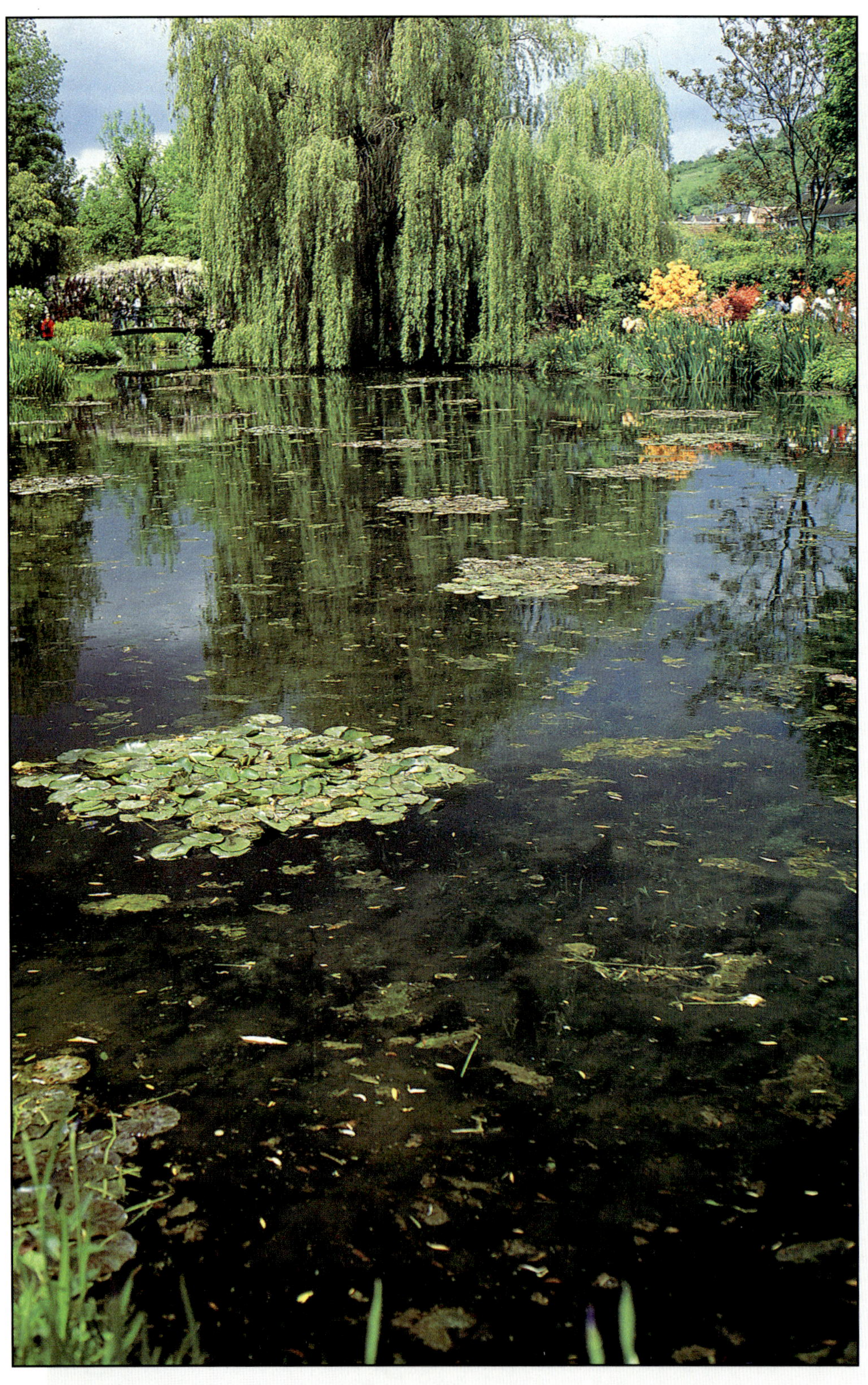

Monet's water gardens at Giverny.

Paris, dimanche 21 mai

Paris, Sunday, May 21st

I walked down to the river Seine at the Alma bridge, where the *bateau mouche* (river cruise boat) was just about to leave. Perfect timing—I had no idea when the next one was departing. I took a lot of pix as is typical when I am around water. I had lunch at a nearby café called the Grand Corona—tomato, mozzarella, and basil salad, and a shrimp cocktail that was really their version of shrimp salad with the pink mayonnaise and ketchup sauce.

My waitress was *si gentile* (very kind). I really wasn't used to all that smiling from a French person, but it was welcome and reminded me of home. Unlike Americans, French people are not taught from birth to smile wherever they go in public, and sometimes I forget this and find myself smiling at all the stessed out faces in the subway. Naturally, I catch myself and stop as I look into eyes that think I'm crazy.

The walk back to the flat, combined with the food I had just enjoyed, made me sleepy, so I retired for a nap. At the same moment, Mom telephoned. She was fine, but she said she was going to have to have an operation some time in July.

Après le repos (After the nap), I walked a long way towards the Brasserie Flo, but I was literally running a little late, *alors*, I found a taxi. Good thing too, because the restaurant is *si difficile* (hard) to find. Flo is on the *cour des Petites Ecuries*, not the *rue des Petites Ecuries*, and the *cour* (alley) is a one way street for those who arrive by car. Many people on their first visit go to the *rue* before the *cour*. (On the way to Flo, I was walking down *avenue Hoche*, and in front of a building was a camel in full dress. Yes, a camel in Paris. Wild, *non*?)

The couple beside me looked friendly, so I struck up a conversation. I found out they were from Alabama and had lived in my hometown of Greensboro for many years!

For *mon dîner* (my dinner) I had a *Kir Royal*, fresh steamed asparagus in *mousselline* sauce (a light Hollandaise sauce), the French version of *chateaubriand*, (a simple grilled filet of beef), and what is always served with steak—french fries *sans* (without) ketchup. Heaven forbid! By the way, deep frying potatoes is a Belgian invention, so they should change the name to Belgian fries—then again, maybe not! I chose a nice light *pinot noir d'Alsace* to accompany this meal, and my choice of three *sorbets* came with the menu—green apple, banana, mango,

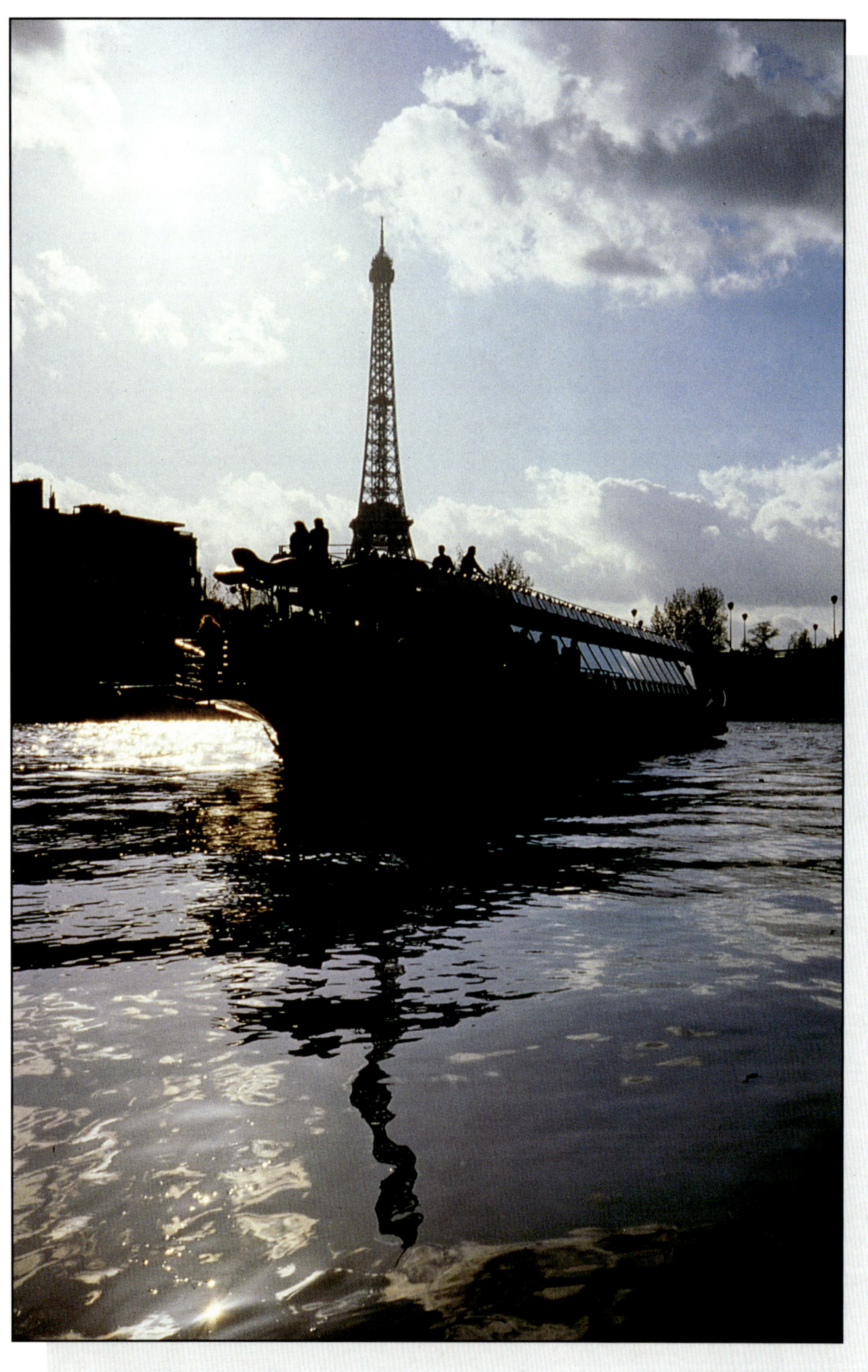

A Bateau Mouche interrupts the reflection of the Eiffel Tower.

and guava. Meals like this one deserve a good cigar, and I had brought one, a mild smoking Montecristo #4 just for the occasion. Very nice! We strolled through the red light district of Saint-Denis and turned right to head for the *Arc de Triomphe,* the grand landmark near where I live. *Bonne nuit*!

Paris, lundi 22 mai

Paris, Monday, May 22nd

I "metroed" it to *Saint-Germain des Près* and walked to the *Ecole Nationale des Beaux Arts*, the same school Brancusi and many other great artists attended in the past. I had a nice visit with a lady there, and she informed me that at the undergraduate level, no one over twenty-six years of age could study at the school, or in any other university in France for that matter, except in the evenings. In America you can go to college at any age, but we're not in America. Further evidence of *socialisme* in France! The lady said she would send me an updated brochure this fall, which will be nice to have, if not for immediate use, at least for the knowledge of what is offered, and to steer interested people in that direction. Classes are in French, *alors, il faut parler bien français. Comprenez?* (So it's necessary to speak good French. Understand?)

Then I got a cab to la Madeleine near the Gucci store and changed some *cheques de voyage* (traveler's checks). The rate was dropping, 4.70 francs per dollar. You can get a better rate using credit cards, so I always tried to pay with Visa or Amex. Also, always haggle with the exchange person until you get a reasonable rate, but know what a "reasonable" rate is before you do so. How do you do that? I buy the *Herald Tribune*, which writes about everything you may need to know about the news of the world. Other English language newspapers may have exchange rates, but I have not read them.

At *Palais Royal* I took the subway to go to school. Class was a little boring, so I was ready for a good nap afterwards, however, a woman across the building was making so much noise with pots, pans, and some blasted door that I couldn't sleep. Every minute or so she would slam the door and keep me from my dreams, dreams of Paris in springtime.

Alors, I got up and decided to have an *Américano*. The café was almost full, and I was lucky enough to get an outdoor table beside an old woman and her dog. My first reaction was to pet it, but I quickly remembered that I was in France, where animal *comportement* (behavior) can be a little different. I waited for my cue, which I encouraged by offering a peanut. *Le chien* (The dog) responded, ate the salty nut, and I made two friends at once. The lady, who lived *juste en haut* (just above), was very kind, just like her *chien*. We spoke about—what else—*la plus belle ville du monde* (the most beautiful city in the world)—Paris. I wanted to tell her all about *Caroline du Nord* (North Carolina), but she kept right on talking about *les monuments, La Seine, et les cafés, bien sur*. She sounded like me when

I tell my friends why I love Paris so. Meanwhile the dog was begging for more food, and the woman looked at me as if to say, "Well you created this problem, now you solve it." It was as if we knew each other; she treated me like she might treat a son. I could tell by the wag in his tail that Sigmund the dog was happy when he left the café that day. So was I.

We ate dinner a little earlier than usual, because I was going to see *Immortal Beloved* on the *Champs*. The movie was excellent! I love films of times long ago like *Amadeus* and this one. *Bonne nuit*!

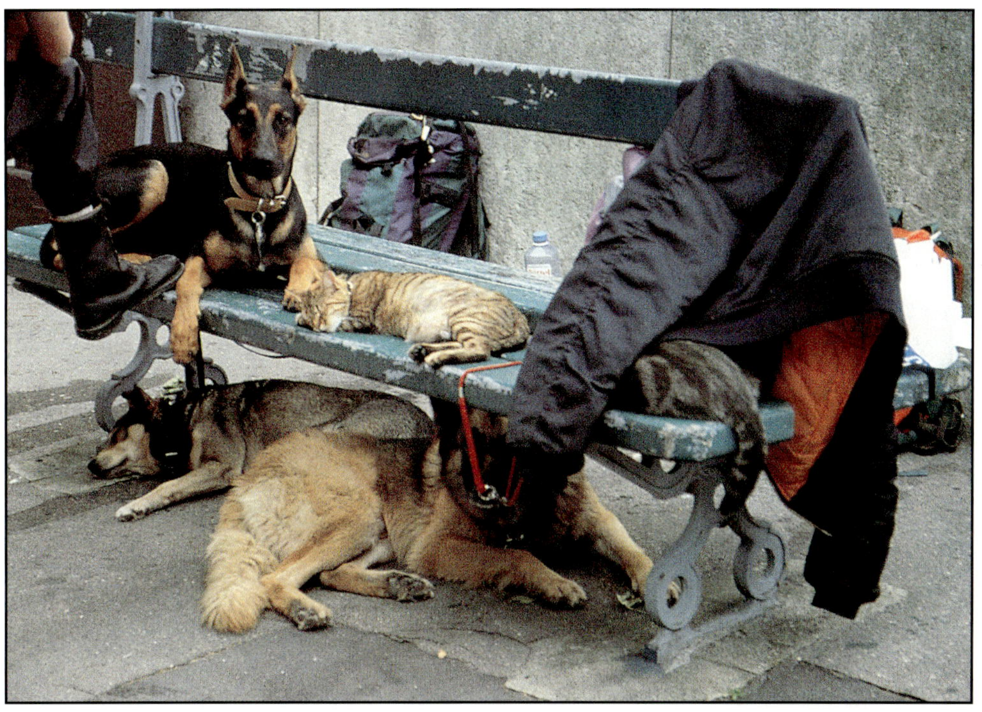

Find all the dogs and cats in this picture!

Paris, mardi 23 mai

Paris, Tuesday, May 23rd

Early on I did some shopping at and around the huge department store *Samaritaine* on the *Rive Droite* (Right Bank) at the *Pont Neuf*, oddly enough, the oldest bridge in Paris. They have almost everything you need, only you have to find it, and without a generous command of the language, *bonne chance* (good luck)! It's not that some French don't speak English. Some do, but often you have to plead your case for what you want before being waited on. And if, by chance, you speak enough French to ask for the item or items, often the response is in "hyperFrench," which can only be understood by some of their family members and close friends.

Then there are the three "*Nons*." In France, when you ask for something it is very important to know beforehand if you can actually obtain it. In other words, you must do your research. If not, then you will walk away feeling helpless after the first "*Non*." Do not fret! The first "*Non*" means, "Why should I sell you something? You're an *étranger* (foreigner) and I've never seen you before." Ask again with more conviction! The second "*Non*" means, "Change my mind if you're sure about what you're looking for." By this time, most anglophones have made it to the nearest exit, but the persistent traveler can survive in France. The last "*Non*" means, "Ask me one more time, and I'll rephrase your request in my own words so as to understand you and find exactly what you are looking for." This is France! Strangers here are strange to the locals, and thus they are treated like strangers. Call it a silly, rude or unfriendly game, but here it's real life. A non-French speaker can get past the three "*nons*" with a prior knowledge of what he can in fact get, and of course with a bilingual native on his side. Otherwise, it's not much different from being in the provinces of China or India. If you are going to play their game, you have to play by their rules *point* (period).

After being waited on, I purchased an Adidas bag and took the *métro* home to get my books. On the way to school I stopped for my ritual *café espresso* at *le zinc* of a nearby *café*. If I open a restaurant in the States, it's going to be called "Le Zinc," named after the bar counters in cafés all over France.

After class I went to *La Poste* for some 4f30 *timbres* (stamps) and then to Virgin Megastore for some CDs. Music in France is outrageously expensive: compact discs cost around thirty dollars each and cassettes cost more than twenty dollars, but if I want good French tunes I must *acheter en France* (buy them in France). Unfortunately, we only get the dregs of foreign music in music stores across America.

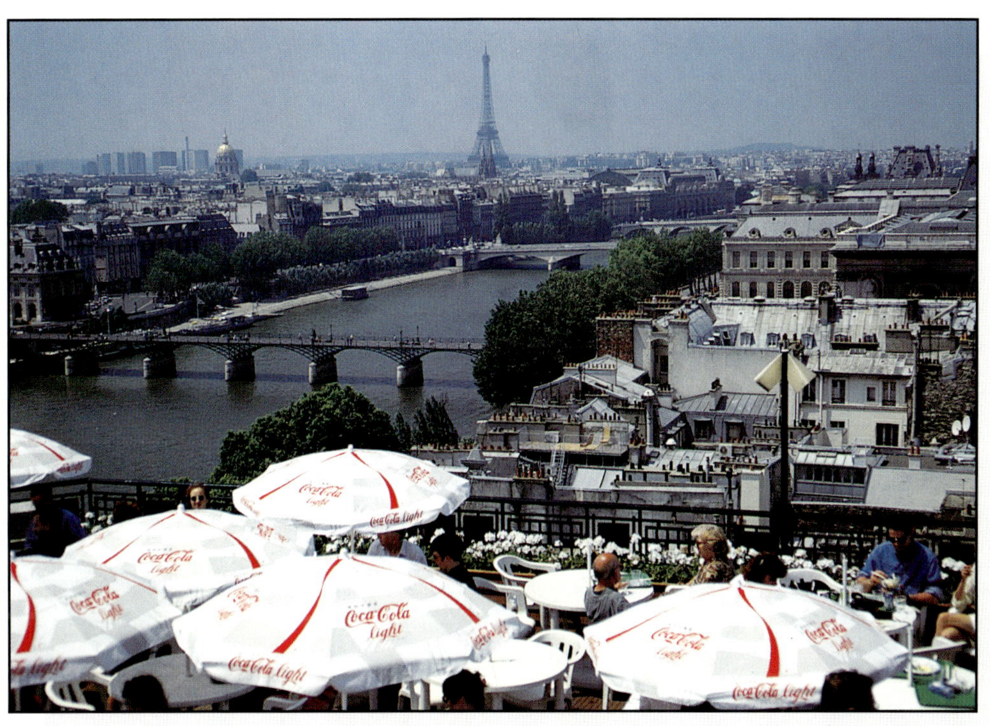

A view from the Samaritaine department store near the Pont Neuf.

On my way home I stopped by Le Garage, a cool clothing store that sells beautiful shirts and belts *de qualité* (of quality), and met Serge, who seemed at the outset much too open-minded and friendly to be French. Don't get me wrong! The French are only *froid* (cold) until you get to know them, at which time they can become your friend for life. Turns out that he was Americanized during his college years in New York.

Around 19h00 I changed, took the *métro* to *La Gare Saint-Lazare*, the train to *Bois Colombes*, and then walked down *rue des Bourguignons* to Thierry and Karine's. I punched *le code*, they buzzed the door from on high, and I climbed the steps to their new flat. *Comme d'habitude* (as usual), the poodle went nuts and wouldn't stop barking until it was safe from "the stranger." I met my two newlywed friends when they were attending UNC-Wilmington in 1993, and we have been friends ever since. We started with a glass of *Pineau de Charentes rouge* for an *apéritif*, followed by *foie gras de canard* (duck foie gras), chicken, broccoli (believe it or not, a new vegetable in France), a *plateau de fromages*, ice cream with fresh pineapple, and of course, *le vin*. Thierry opened a bottle of their wedding *champagne*, which added to our delight in what was a perfect evening. We called it a night, and Thierry gave me a ride back in to town. Luckily I wasn't driving, because I was still under the influence of French hospitality. A *demain*!

Paris, mercredi 24 mai

Paris, Wednesday, May 24th

Slept fairly late due to the night before; had my ritual café at *Le Hoche* and went to class. We talked about the DELF examination, which is an exam to test a foreigner's overall fluency in the language and knowledge of French culture. *En septembre* I would sit for the first four sections of the test in Vichy at a wonderful language school called CAVILAM (*Centre Audiovisuel International Des Langues Modernes*). I would not be allowed to take the other two sections until the next examination period.

I had to go cigar shopping, so I metroed to *Le Boulmich*, where the two saints, Michel and Germain, come together. From there, if you walk towards *Saint-Germain des Près*, there will be a cigar shop on your right. Let me warn you *que c'est très cher* (it's expensive), but where else can an *Américain* find a real Cuban cigar? Five Montecristo #4s cost 210FF everywhere you go in France. I couldn't believe that in the provinces cigars would be also *si cher* (so expensive). They

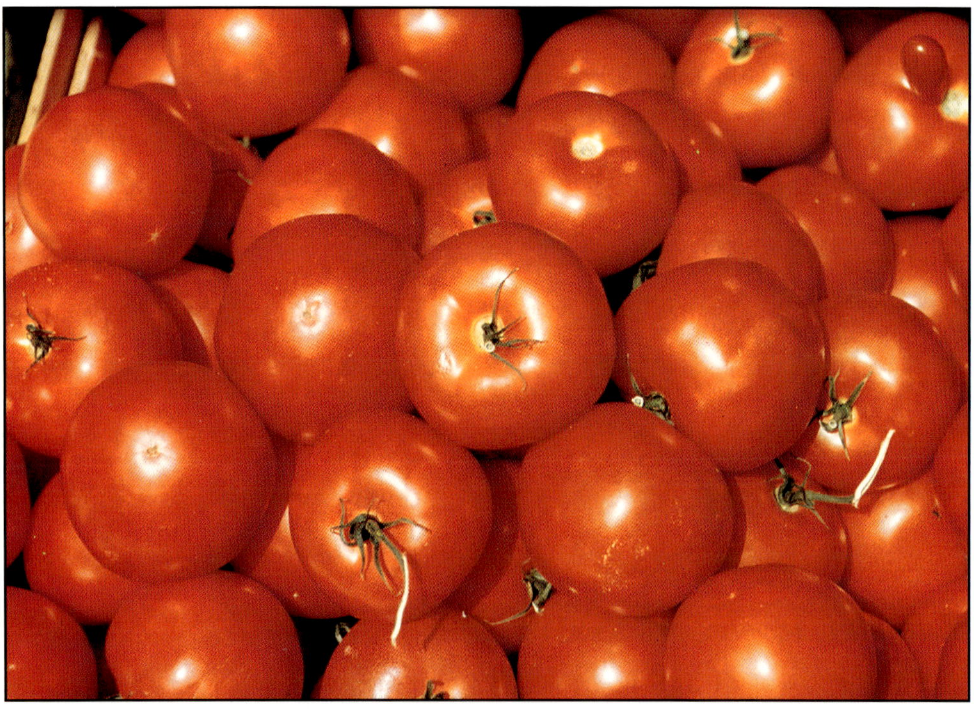

The colors of a French market are a feast for the eyes as well as the stomach.

are, *alors*, there must be some kind of price control going on. *Malheureusement*, haggling is out of the question with tobacco products, *d'ailleurs* (besides), the *tabacs* (tobacco stores) are already too crowded with customers waiting to buy cigarettes.

Many French would have a hard time graduating from American marketing schools, because it appears they do not like to sell, possibly due to the fact that most are generally not concerned with whether you buy or not. Sometimes when I walk into a clothing shop I feel like I am intruding on some important meeting. It's simple! The customer is NOT king in France. Ever since I've been coming to France, I hear that there is such an economic crisis and that no one is buying anything, but when I see that shopkeepers would rather sell a few items at exorbitantly high prices, than sell many for a little less, it's no wonder. Did you know that there are some cafés and restaurants charging between six and eight dollars for one eleven-ounce beer? To this observation, my French friends respond that French people don't want to work any more than they have to. Maybe so, but here we are talking more logic, not more work.

France likes to exaggerate and has always considered itself on the edge of some kind of economic, social, or political disaster, and I'm never surprised when one of my French friends makes some kind of pessimistic remark about something his or her countrymen or country is doing. My friend Delphine, whom I met at the *Au Bon Marché* department store last trip, believes that there is enough work in France for all who truly desire to work and that the problem of *chomage* (unemployment) is only caused by those who will not work or who have stopped trying. And the weather! The French, like most of us, love to complain about *le temps* (the weather), and it's true that they get more annual rainfall in Paris than in London, but the weather is always on their minds.

In the future, I'll try not to generalize and stereotype a people who, despite their peculiar mentality, always seem to please us in the end.

That night we went to see *La Cité des Enfants Perdus*, a bizzare yet entertaining film about a mad scientist who kidnaps children and steals their dreams. I found it hard to understand, yet entertaining all the while because the main character, "Juan," was Ron Pearlman—an American. A *demain*!

Paris, jeudi 25 mai

Paris, Thursday, May 25th

La pluie!

I went to La Muette *métro* stop and walked with some fellow Americans to the *Musée Marmottan*, where many of Monet's works are simply yet beautifully displayed. It's a rather quaint and laid-back museum compared to the large national ones, and you can even have a comfortable seat and admire the lily pads, or, like one gentleman I saw, catch up on some "Zs."

For lunch I stopped in a *patisserie* with seating for a quick bite. I had *une salade frisée aux lardons* (frizzy lettuce and chunks of bacon in a vinaigrette sauce), and an Orangina for eleven bucks, which is *pas mal* (not bad) for Paris.

There is a potential great shot of *La Tour Eiffel* near the corner of *rue Saint-Dominique* and the *Boulevard de la Tour Maubourg*. One day I'll go back there.

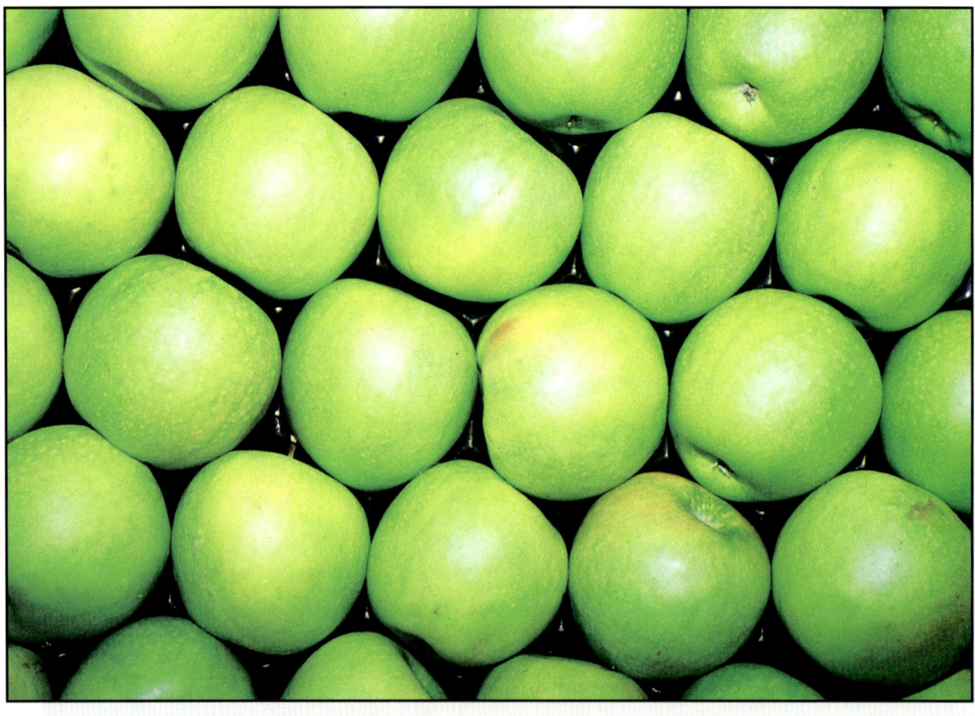

Fruit and vegetable vendors often make beautiful displays worth a shot.

Today it was overcast and I was headed home via *Les Champs, alors* that *photo* will have to wait.

Since Jeanne-Marie was out with friends, we had cold cuts and a salad for dinner—sort of a change, but it was good. For dessert we had cantaloupe, Hawaiian arabica coffee, and a cigar. Like most young Europeans, Claudia and Miriam smoke cigarettes, but they are always considerate of others in the room. *Moi*, I would never smoke a cigar if anyone in the room objected, if there was poor ventilation, or if there were any children around. This is not the way things work in France. French people smoke everywhere: in cafés, on the street, in fine restaurants, in the car, on the train, in a plane, and above all, in the night clubs. Now you may be thinking that everyone else does that too. True, but in France there is no escape from *la fumée* (smoke) of burning tobacco unless you stay at home and sit in your room all day. I smell cigarette smoke even on the sidewalk quite often. And many of the old cafés and *restos* in France have poor ventilation, so naturally they fill up with smoke. The bottom line is this, no one has the right to subject another to a substance which can be harmful to his or her health without that person's consent, *non*? Enough seriousness! *Salut*!

Paris, vendredi 26 mai

Paris, Friday, May 26th

Breakfast was the usual hot tea with milk and *tartines*. Beautiful day! First I mailed a box of French magazines to the U.S., *par avion économique*, and took a taxi with my "traveling companion" to the *rue de* Levis to shoot the street market there. It was supposed to be one of Paris' best, but I found otherwise. Everyone seemed so paranoid of my camera. I guess that's understandable in a city where some "bad apples" take advantage of others. At any rate, I got a lot of cold stares from people who must have their reasons.

L*e déjeuner* (Lunch) was at the Hippopotamus, an always-packed French version of an American steak house. J*'ai mangé* (I ate) the vegetable *terrine* with tomato *coulis* (purée of fruit or vegetables) and medallions of duck. D*élicieux*! Later, I packed *mes valises* (my suitcases) for the two-hour train ride to Nantes, making sure to get my laundry that was hanging from *le truc* in the kitchen. A *truc* is anything in the universe that you don't have a name for—we Americans and British use the word thing or thingamajig. The French have another word for "thing,"

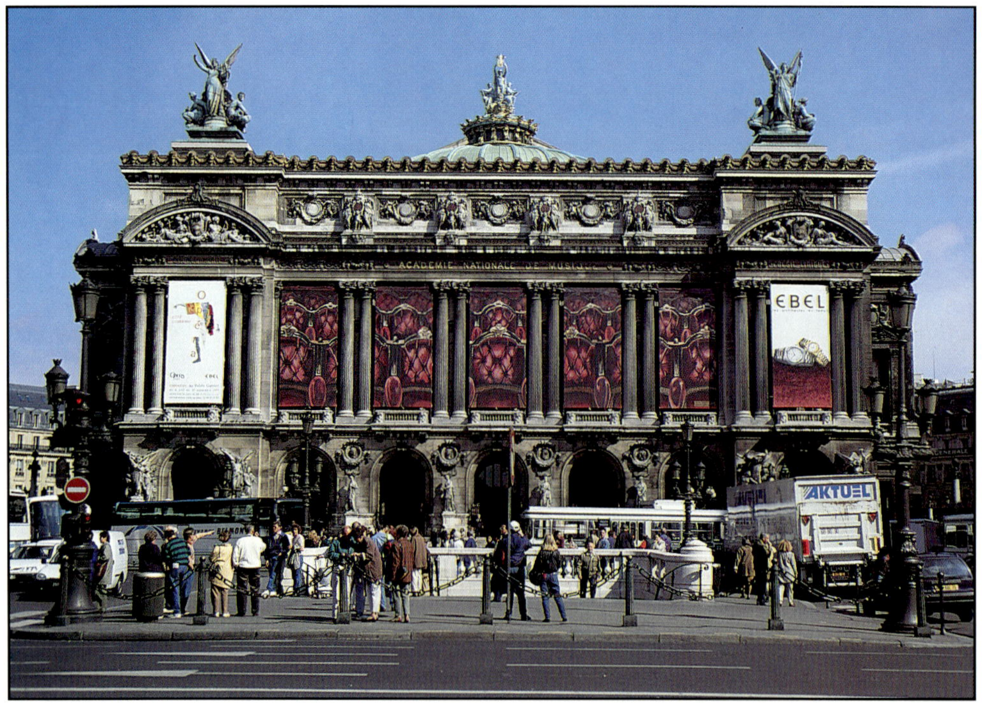

The old Opéra Garnier in the first arrondissement.

marchand, which can be used in a mildly derogatory manner in the expression, "*une espece de marchand*," which means "some sort of something."

Since I had a fairly copious lunch, I decided to eat light for dinner. After walking for about an hour I arrived at L'*Opéra de Paris* where there is a *grand café* called *Café de la Paix*. It was crowded, but I found a table outside with a view of the *Opéra* and all the people passing by. I had a smoked salmon sandwich with Ceylan tea, and a *Coupe de la Paix*, which is vanilla, hazelnut, and coconut ice creams, *mousse au chocolat*, *meringue*, cigarette cookies, *chantilly*, and nougat sauce. So much for eating light!

In Paris, even though I'm often alone, I don't feel alone, possibly because there are people everywhere I go, and because I either have my "traveling companion" during the day or my journal to write in at night. It is a common sight to see people dining or having coffee alone in the big city, and tourists can easily be spotted writing *cartes postales* or in their *journaux intimes* (diaries).

My African cab driver was quite animated as he explained to me that his daughter was on a scholarship to Boston University and that she spoke English like an American. I was impressed, but more impressed by this man's youthfulness. He looked like he was my age, but he told me he was fifty-four. Tomorrow's a new day!

Lorient, samedi 27 mai

Lorient, Saturday, May 27th

My natural alarm clock woke me at 5h30 to get ready to catch *le train* at *La Gare Montparnasse*. Luckily, I did not have far to carry my bags to a taxi stand, which is the best place to get a cab in Paris. There, the taxis line up, and, *normalement* (normally), the client will take the first cab in the cue, but I recently heard that you can take any one you want. This is not the truth! Drivers respect the rights of one another, and it would be very bad to take another's customer.

I arrived an hour before departure, as is my preference, and read a magazine while I sat on my baggage near the tracks. Unusually for a Friday, the train was not full, so I was able to sit where I wanted. Trains in France run on monochronic time—in other words, "on time." The SNCF (*Société Nationale des Chemins de Fer*), is one of, if not the most, advanced and efficient railway systems in the world today, with its super high speed TGV (*Train à Grande Vitesse*), and chunnel trains. In Nantes I caught another cab for the airport to pick up my rental car, and once again I was early. A little over an hour later a man brought me a tiny red Peugeot 106 fresh from the factory. I signed my life away and drove off—destination: the port of Lorient via Vannes. When I arrived it was lunchtime, *alors*, Philippe and Ann-Marie were home from where they work across the street. They own and manage a small women's *haute couture* clothing boutique, the only one in a town of eighty thousand *habitants*. Philippe *et moi* had a *café* before he returned to work, and I headed for "*une crêperie par excellence*" according to my friend.

The Saint-Georges had the typical Brittany *crêperie* ambiance with wooden chairs, walls, and tables, but the high ceilings were a slight twist. My first *crêpe* was *salé*, which means salty, and made from *blé noir*, or buckwheat. It had an egg sunny-side up, ham shoulder, shredded emmenthal cheese, and tomato sauce. Dessert, a *crêpe sucré* (sweet crêpe), was a white flour pancake with pears, vanilla ice cream, hot chocolate sauce, and *chantilly*. My favorite! The owner gave me a menu for a *souvenir*, and I left with a smile on *mon visage* (my face).

It was time for a haircut, so I found a place nearby and put my life on the line for the second time in one day. It's funny how I'm always a little apprehensive about allowing someone to cut *mes cheveux* (my hair) in France. Not that I have any cause for fear; the French probably invented *les ciseaux* (scissors). Part of it must be the infinite language barrier which exists, no matter how well one

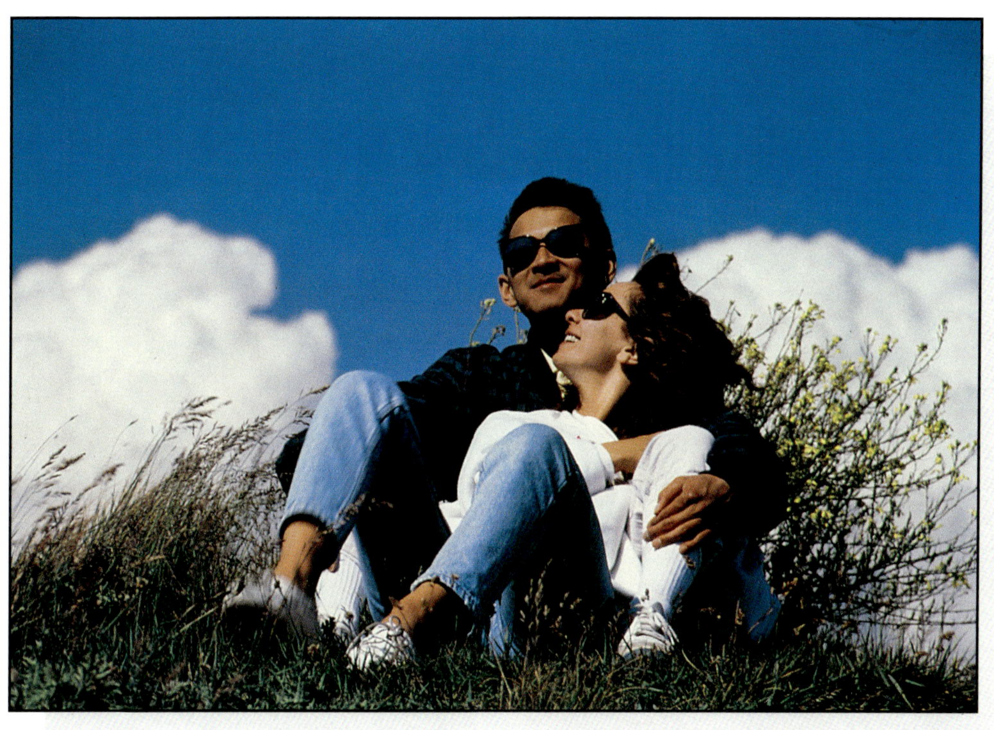

Philippe and Anne-Marie near Lorient.

speaks the other's native tongue, and the other part is the question in an American's mind, "Does this person have something against foreigners?" Thus far, all of these fears are unfounded, I am happy to say, and once again I got a good haircut.

Philippe came home and we drove to his parent's restaurant to pick up our Chinese dinner that Madame Truong was preparing while we enjoyed a Chinese *apéritif* called Kuei Hua Chen Chiew (don't try to say it on a full stomach). We ate like kings and queens as we enjoyed the wonderful food and my gift, a bottle of *Margaux*. For dessert we had *Saint-Honorés*, which are puff pastries with fresh fruit, burnt sugar, or *caramel*, and *chantilly*. Delicious and light! After dinner Philippe and I went for a cruise to the beach where the air was so fresh with the scent of marine life that it reminded me of home. *Bonne nuit*! *Dors bien*!

Rochefort, dimanche 28 mai

Rochefort, Sunday, May 28th

Today is France's Mother's Day—*La Fête des Mères*. All the *magasins* (shops) have signs in their windows announcing this wonderful day to appreciate *les mères françaises* (French mothers) with a gift. We had breakfast and prepared to drive to the Chateau Talhouet, a sixteenth-century Breton manor house set in a fifty-acre park on the edge of the Lanvaux moors. It overlooks the small Arz valley and sandstone hills of Rochefort en terre.

For lunch we drove to Rochefort for some *crêpes* and hard apple cider, which can be a delightful low-alcohol beverage called *cidre doux*, or a stronger carbonated brew called *cidre bouché brut*. We enjoyed the former while their son, Arnaud, who I call a two and a half year old "wild man," drank apple juice. My *crêpe salé* (here they call them "*galettes de blé noir*") had onions, mushrooms, ham, cheese, and tomatoes. The main problem with some *crêperies* is that orders are usually ready at different times, and since *crêpes* must be served hot, right off

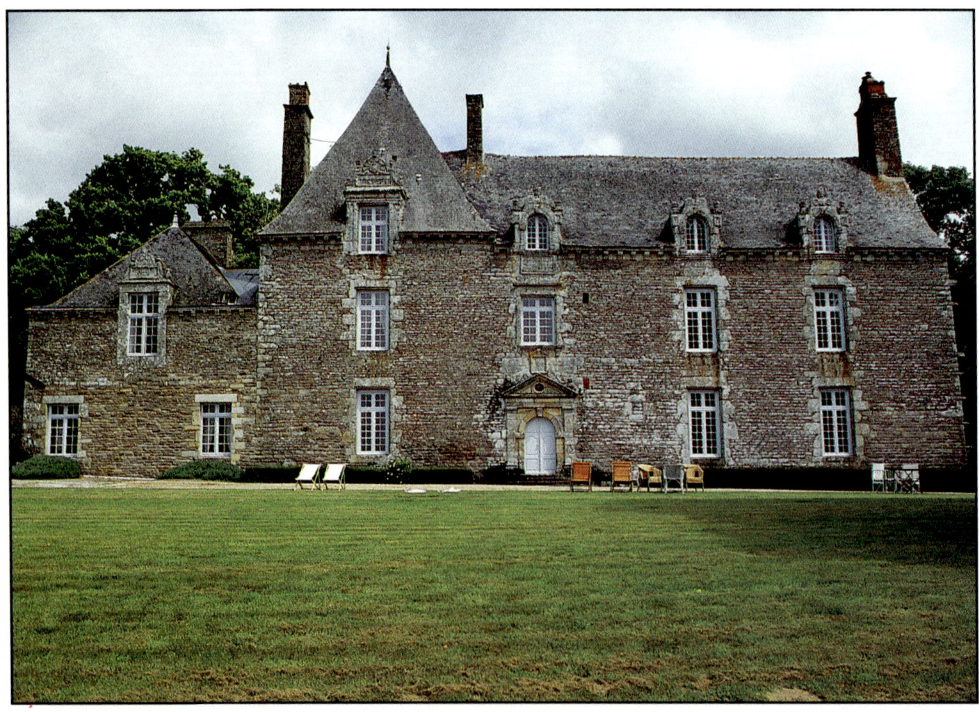

Chateau Talhouet

the *plaque*, people at the same table can end up eating at different times, as was the case here.

A chateau is a great place to relax, and we took every advantage of this by napping and walking through the woods and garden to the ancient *église* (church), and laying out in the sun on the terrace overlooking the plush green valley stretching out as far as the eye can see. Ah, *la France*! Philippe and Ann-Marie come often to the Talhouet, so they prepared me for *une soirée gastronomique* (a gastronomic evening). We began with a *coup de champagne*, a delight that most Americans miss out on, possibly because it's not our custom. When was the last time you had a champagne cocktail at a friend's home or *au restaurant*? The entrée was *langoustines* (Dublin Bay prawns) in a cream sauce, and the *plat principal* was cabbage leaves stuffed with veal, pork, and beef with a *boeuf bourguignon* sauce. Our host brought out a selection of divine cheeses from the region, but we were not through yet. Dessert! We had a hot *soufflé* of chocolate pudding sitting in a pool of *crème anglaise*, a different twist from the light and airy *soufflés* made predominantly from egg whites—a delectable meal, but no cigars, because I had left them back in Lorient. I'll probably quit smoking soon. *Au lit*!

Port Louis, lundi 29 mai

Port Louis, Monday, May 29th

Something I love about France is that *le petit déjeuner* can always be served in the room, so you can have that first cup of strong arabica almost before getting out of bed. The ultimate continental breakfast for me is *brioche, croissants,* toast, Brittany or Normandy butter, jams, yogurt, fresh-squeezed orange juice, and that energizing black stuff. The Talhouet served just that, and I enjoyed every bite while watching French music videos—it was a long weekend, and besides, you're supposed to lounge around in an old *chateau*!

La pluie was coming down when we departed, keeping with the norm for Breton weather. We stopped by *McDoe* on the way back, and Arnaud had a sort of Happy Meal, while I ate a shrimp and salmon salad with delicious ketchup and mayo cocktail sauce and a Coke. Why doesn't McDonald's in the U.S. have things like that, and fruit cocktail, beer, wine, espresso? Maybe one day.

My friends went to the *boutique* while I drove to Port Louis for some pix. Apart from the old fort and some peaceful boats, there was *pas grandes choses* (not a lot) to photograph. Monsieur et Madame Truong invited us to dinner at the restaurant, and it was delicious—Vietnamese fried chicken, shrimp and snow peas, called "*mange tout*" in French, I guess because you're supposed to eat the whole thing, and sticky rice. A chilled gewertztraminer went nicely with everything, including the mocha almond cake Madame made just for the occasion. Once back at Phil's, we enjoyed a *petit tisan* (hot herbal beverage), and went to bed.

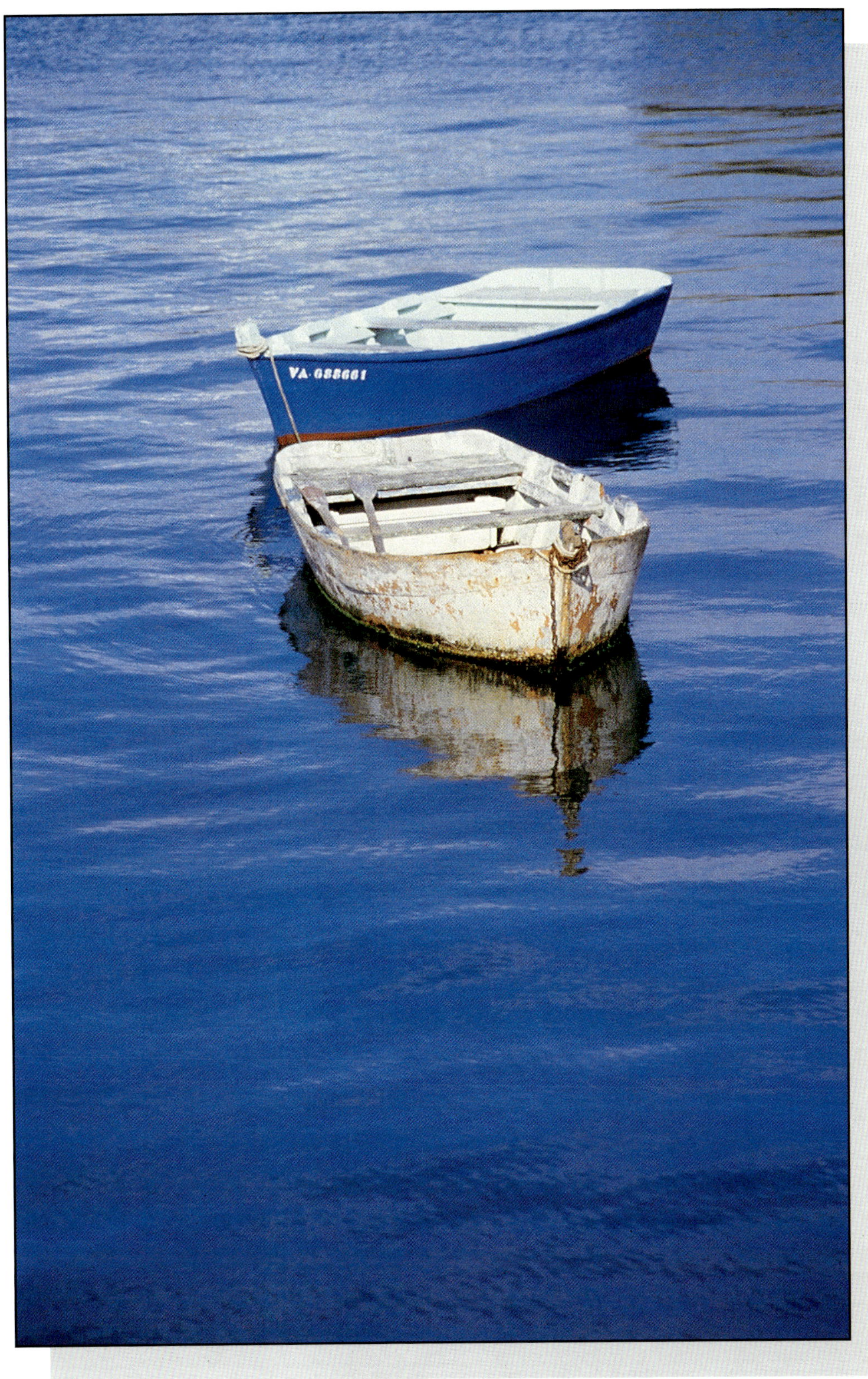

*Two boats keep each other company
on these still waters of Port Louis.*

Saint-Malo, mardi 30 mai

Saint-Malo, Tuesday, May 30th

Got up early and drove the "little red wagon" to Saint-Malo, finding the hotel *Le Korrigane* without even asking for directions. In a city that's divided into several smaller *quartiers*, Saint-Servan being the principal one, I was grateful for my good fortune. Two men greeted me, and I left my bags in the little room *en bas* (downstairs), only taking my camera equipment and a raincoat. Although, the room was *petite*, it did have a bathtub, toilet, mini bar, television with *Canal Plus*, and doors opening into the garden.

I forgot about the room for a while and headed for Le Mont Saint-Michel, a convenient forty-five minute drive away. The place has a special kind of energy in the air, the site of loads of *histoire* (history) that makes France such a wonderful destination today. Sure there are lots of cars, tour buses, and tourists, but this kind of world apart guards a secret from those who will not see. It's everywhere from the road leading to it, where sheep look for greener pastures, to

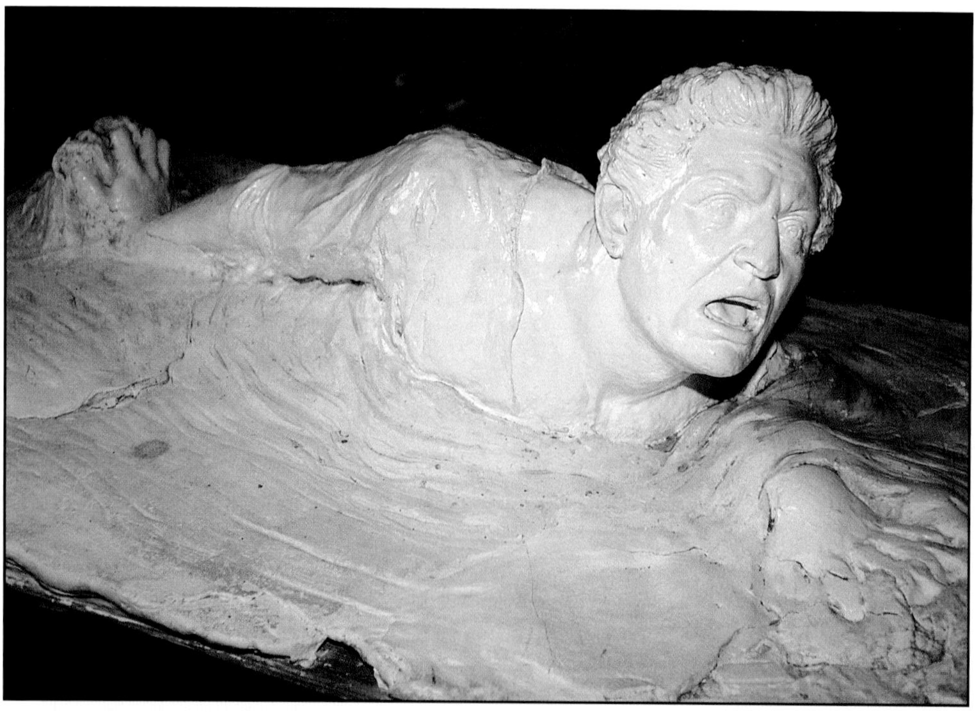

A museum statue showing the danger of the quicksands surrounding Le Mont Saint-Michel.

the crooked climbing streets where locals sell their wares, to the perilous quicksand sandbars which hide from the foolhardy, to the fishermen, to the unmistakable spire of the cathedral that seems to signal out to all parts, to Mère Poulard who owns an outrageously expensive restaurant and half of all the commerce there, and finally to the tide, that *marée* that takes a matter of minutes to rise above the sandy shoals, making it dangerous to be where I was when I took some of my best pictures. No worries! My watch was working, and I knew when the next tide would come in. The *Mont*, known as *la merveille* (the marvel), is magnificent. It rises up and up from the shifting sands, with buildings on its back, until it reaches for and touches the heavens with a golden angel.

I, being the "typical tourist" that I can be sometimes, dined at Mère Poulard, where an artisan-made plain *omelette* costs around thirty dollars. For that, you're paying for the show and the sounds of the chef beating the eggs, which I photographed earlier that afternoon. Many celebrities have eaten there, sending autographed pictures or movie posters that are now prominently displayed on the restaurant's walls. Now one more has eaten there (just a joke)!

I had lamb medallions, with veggies and apples, of all things. In France, dessert is part of any well-balanced meal, *alors*, I ordered the cinnamon-soaked peeled pear in caramel sauce with orange sections and *sabayon* sauce soaking the plate, which took longer to make than my main course, but, boy, it was good. I made it back to Saint-Malo in thirty minutes and crashed for the night. Pray for good weather tomorrow!

Le Mont Saint-Michel, mercredi 31 mai

Le Mont Saint-Michel, Wednesday, May 31st

Up at the crack of dawn, *petit déjeuner* in my *chambre*, and off to Le Mont Saint-Michel for another adventure, but this time in the clouds. Oh well! A *cause du temps* (Because of the weather), I stayed indoors and did all the museums, then had a marvelous lunch at a surprisingly reasonable price. I had *langoustines*, with homemade mayonnaise, poached salmon with mussels, baby shrimp, mushrooms, and dessert *bien sur*. But before the sweets, I was served a plate of *fromages* that almost put me over the edge, but who could ever pass up a small bowl of tantalizing *mousse au chocolate* to top off even a copious meal? *Délicieux*! I was stuffed yet pleased.

Just as I was leaving the restaurant, the sun appeared, and I walked all over the island-like place taking *encore des photos* (more pictures). As I was driving away from the *Mont*, sheep were crossing the road, so I quickly pulled over and started snapping. From that angle the sun ducked partially behind the clouds, allowing me a beautiful, macabre shot of the majestic and mysterious world I was leaving behind.

In Saint-Malo I did my laundry at a nearby *laverie* before setting out to the harbor at Saint-Servan for more photo opportunities. Then it was back to my room to get ready for the evening. I stumbled upon a local dive, and as I sipped my *Américano*, I chatted with the owner and her client friend. They advised me that "my" restaurant, the one I was supposed to go to, was closed, *alors*, they made reservations for me at another just up the street and gave me a card, good for one free glass of champagne at the restaurant. Why not take a chance? So I had another drink, thanked the ladies, and shoved off to discover truly something special. *Au PierAlain* has six small tables, enough room for sixteen persons maximum, one clean bathroom, a minuscule bar counter complete with tulip champagne glasses, a refrigerator, a wine rack, and a kitchen big enough for the one chef, who is part owner, Pier. Alain, server, bartender, and part owner, was *super sympa* (very nice), and introduced me to his brown dachshund in the chair in front of me as he handed me a glass of bubbly. It was completely amazing! PierAlain was a lesson in hospitality. The food was good without much of a wait, other tables were ordering sundaes and banana splits for dessert and espresso, yet not a soul was complaining about service. My dinner was quite nice—fish *terrine* with toast points and the homemade mayonnaise-based cocktail sauce, *langoustines* with mayo, and blueberry and raspberry sherbet.

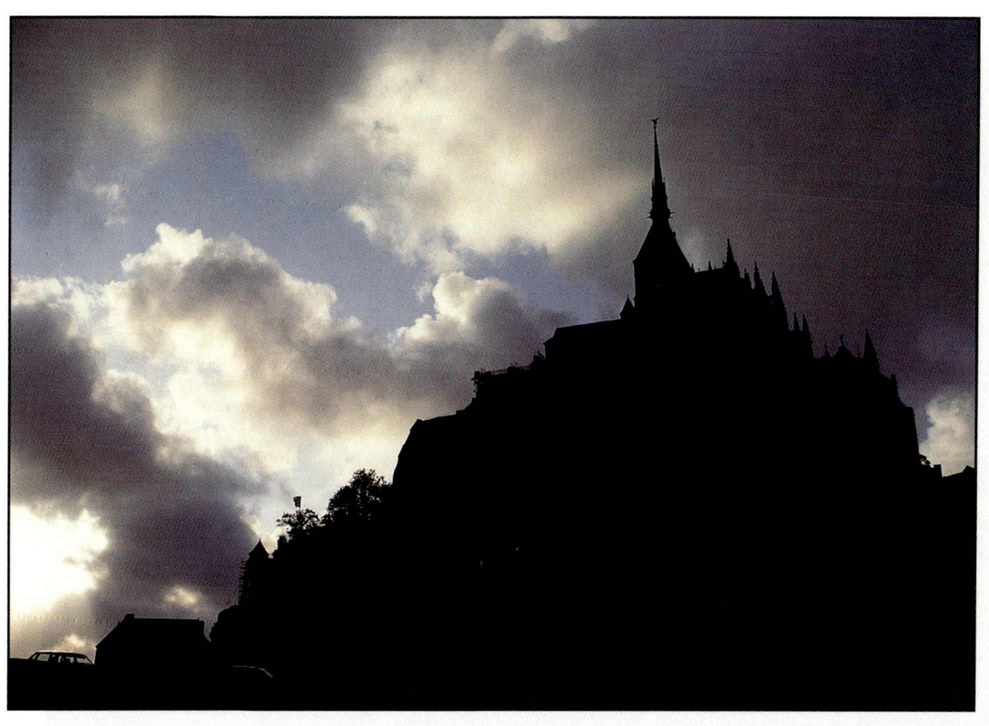

The familiar silhouette of Le Mont Saint-Michel.

Being the curious type, I inquired about the music, and Alain asked me to wait a minute. He proceeded to make a phone call, and we waited until a beautiful woman with strawberry hair walked in the door. Alain handed me the cassette box and this *française's* picture was on the cover! Turns out that Michelle sings and performs theater in and around Saint-Malo, waiting on thirsty Frenchmen at the bar across the street during the off-season. *Elle est très gentile* (She is very nice). My new friends toasted me with two more free *verres de champagne,* and I bought one of Madame Danner's cassettes.

I've always dreamed of having my own restaurant. I imagine this delightful continental gathering place will serve fish *terrine* and shrimp with creamy cocktail sauce, smoked Scotch salmon, melon with Parma ham, roast leg of lamb, *rotisserie* free-range chicken, *filet mignon,* fresh fish with cream sauces, special exotic fruit creations, and of course, sumptuous salads, from *niçoise* to Caesar. The restaurant will be a kind of *brasserie/crêperie,* have excellent beers, excellent wines, excellent food, excellent service, excellent music, excellent atmosphere, and excellent desserts. A zinc bar counter could add to the ambience as well. *On verra* (We'll see)!

Cancale & La Houle, jeudi 1 juin

Cancale & La Houle, Thursday, June 1st

I drove to Cancale and La Houle, where I walked around and found a *pharmacie* so I could buy aspirin for my sore throat. Probably just a common cold—no big deal. Then I drove along the coast to *Les Rochers Sculptés*, where the nineteenth-century Abbot Foure sculpted larger-than-life faces and animals in the rocks on the face of a cliff overlooking the sea. This was definitely a photo op. Janvier and his wife, who own the restaurant and *faïence* shop (hand-crafted and hand-painted earthenware), were very kind. *Je suis curieux, alors,* (Since I was curious) I discovered that one of the more attractive lines of *faïence* did not yet have representation in the U.S.—another business opportunity for somebody. Lunch outside by the cliffs and the sea was just what the doctor ordered: smoked salmon and creamed goat cheese salads, both on toasted country bread with fresh cream for the *saumon fumé* (smoked salmon). *Très leger et délicieux* (very light and delicious)! Speaking of dessert, I had scrumptious apple crumble, most likely a *recette* from Old England.

My dream *resto* will serve those very same appetizers/entrées. Character—that's what my restaurant will have. It cannot be cold and uninviting, rather it will be a place where people want to spend time. The walls will speak. The tables, chairs, and tablecloths will sing, and the place settings will evoke emotions of "home." The food will lift spirits, and nourish souls, and the spirits will heal the heart. Even the bathrooms will be a topic of conversation. In the beginning we will serve *crêpes* and one or two complete *menus* (*un menu* is paying one price for a combination of appetizer, entrée, and dessert without beverage, or sometimes just the main course and a dessert). *Crêperie*, wine bar, tea room, piano bar, *brasserie*—at the time of this writing none of these existed in North Carolina, except possibly *brasseries*. Anyway, there are lots of possibilities all over the United States.

In Lorient, Monsieur Truong gave me the phone number for a government-sponsored organization for apprenticeships in the culinary arts, so I called about the *stage de crêperie* (*crêperie* training course). A gentleman informed me about dates, prices, and about several success stories in San Francisco, Saint Louis, and New York.

I took my afternoon tea at the same bar as yesterday. Hey, I'm becoming a local! The music there is good rock and roll, which can be a comfort when you're alone, the nature of an artistic photographer's business. Months ago I

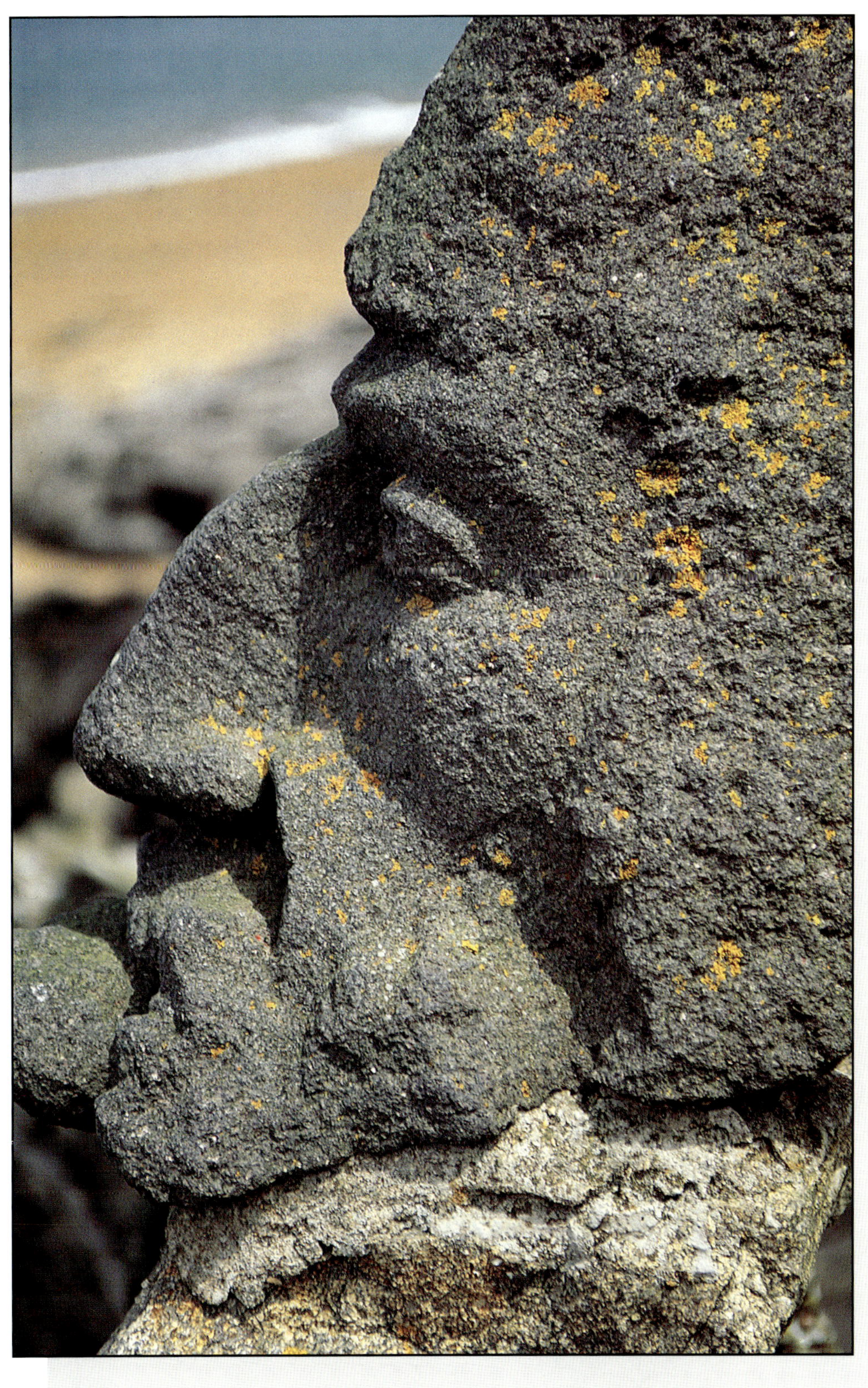

The origin of the expression "stone faced" taken at Les Rochers Sculptés.

had reserved a table at the *Saint-Placide* for dinner through the efforts of the able management of the *Korrigane*. At the risk of getting rained on, I made the fifteen-minute walk to the bright, flowery-decorated restaurant—*tenez* (get this), a porch up against a stone building with sliding glass doors, plexiglass roof, and curtains draping the ceiling to cover the glass. The place has plastic tables and chairs, but they are covered with beautiful tablecloths, and the chairs have comfortable pillows of the same fabric. The porch holds about twelve people. *Ambience est tout* (Ambience is everything)!

First, they offered me *amuse-gueules* (mouth teasers) of *tapenade* (a spread made from anchovies, black olives, olive oil, and garlic), and fresh cream on toast and a cheese puff to "amuse my mouth" before the meal. Along with that I enjoyed a *Kir Royal* with a little twist—Benedictine. *Pas mal* (Not bad)! I was amazed when some folks tried to enter the restaurant with a dog, a common occurrence in this country, but they were told, "*Pas de chiens* (No dogs)." That surprised me, and surprised them even more; they had to go elsewhere. My next course was steamed oysters, *peu cuit* (almost raw), in a simple butter and parsley sauce, which was sublime, and *langoustines* in their shells. Their filet of Saint-Pierre (a small fish), with *ratatouille*, broccoli, and an *espece de marchand* (black pasta noodles I could neither identify nor eat). Dessert made up for that, as they brought me three puff pastries with prune, vanilla, and caramel ice creams and a Gianduja chocolate sauce. Delightfully sinful!

After dinner I went to get Alain, who simply left his restaurant to have a few drinks with Michelle and me across the street. We had *Kir Royals* and listened to my favorite French singer, *Françis Cabrel*, the James Taylor of France. When I told them about my possible apprenticeship in Vannes they said they might come visit me during that time. It was a good long day! A *demain*!

Lorient, vendredi 2 juin

Lorient, Friday, June 2nd

I naturally arose without a wakeup call to take my continental breakfast in the room and watched *Les Actualités* (French news). Loaded the car and headed for Dol de Bretagne, where I met an old woman who allowed me to photograph her house, the cat in the window, the dog, her fish, and her flowers. Since I like flowers, she strongly suggested that I go to a place called Saint-Juvat on my way to Lorient. I set out for this place via Dinan, which wasn't a big deal, at least by car, without stopping, arriving at Saint-Juvat thanks to the directions from the ticket salesperson at *la gare* (train station) in Dinan. No offense, but this little community was a boring dud, with so few houses that they could be counted on three hands, and only a few flower beds here and there. *En ravanche* (on the other hand), the countryside was quite green and beautiful, with farms all around.

I was hungry, so I walked into a *crêperie* where a luncheon party was going on for locals only, but I was unaware of that. You can imagine their reaction when I peeked my head in the room full of people who had probably never seen an American photographer before. After waiting ten minutes at the bar in the next room, I read that the place was open to the public only at night, so I left never having seen a soul that worked there. I was in the middle of nowhere, *vraiment* (truly)!

Before entering the town of Lorient, I drove to the coast to get some shots and to explore a little. The waves were crashing up against the rocks in the surf and the landscape reminded me of California. *Quel beau paysage* (What beautiful landscape)! Although France is only a little larger than the state of Texas, it has one of the most varied topographies of any country in the world, with several major mountain ranges, including the ancient volcanos of Auvergne and of course, the Alps; an ocean; a sea; a channel; splendid navagable rivers; plains; and underground grottos where early man left his unmistakable signature.

Alors, when I arrived *chez* Philippe *et* Ann-Marie, they were ready to *aller au* (to go to the) *restaurant*. The Vivier (Fish Tank) had slow service that night, but the food was good and we were not in a hurry. Jacques, a doctor in Lorient, and his beautiful wife joined us as we were sipping our *apéritifs*, some sort of delicious concoction with fruit juice and champagne. By that time I was starving. We ordered, and waited. And waited. Finally food came, and my Lobster Thermador almost made up for the poor service. Dessert was an irresistable

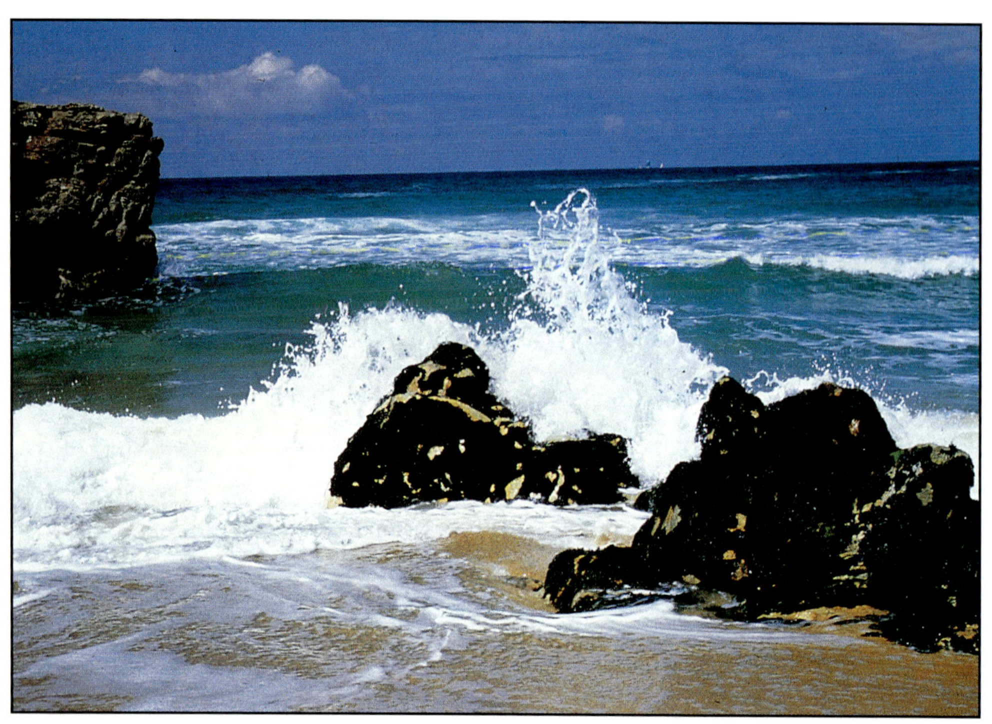

A rocky beach near Lorient.

combination of chocolate mousse spread over layers of sweet biscuit with mocha butter cream and a chocolate *fondant* covering. Heavenly! Naturally, our discussion was mostly about vacations—my friend's trip to Canada this summer and a dream trip in February to Guadeloupe for all of us. They invited me to go along. *On verra*! My new friends invited Philippe and me to his house for an after-dinner drink and to give me some wine from his *cave* (wine-cellar) to take home. I hate to blow all of the stereotypes we Americans have of the French, but this business of rudeness here? It's simply a case of a few "bad apples" spoiling the whole bunch, baby. *Vive la France*! *Bonne nuit*!

Lorient, samedi 3 juin

Lorient, Saturday, June 3rd

First thing in the morning, I walked through the town of Lorient to *La Poste* to mail three boxes—various gifts at just under five kilos, clothing at just over two kilos, and more gifts at under two kilos. According to the postal worker, France no longer has surface mail. That's hard to believe—no more boats? I was told that everything delivered by *La Poste* goes *par avion* (by air). *C'est bête* (That's stupid)! After giving the lady an arm and a leg, over 340FF, I got my bags and dropped the keys off at the *boutique*. I thanked my friends, said *au revoir*, and headed for Nantes, the seventh *plus grande ville* (largest city) in France after Bordeaux. I was very lucky to find #44, rue de la Paix, because there was no #44. Cécile and Laurent live at #14, the code postale is 44000, and somehow I got my numbers mixed up. *C'est pas grave* (No big deal)! Once I was near the house, I remembered vaguely from the year before, when Cécile and I were running around trying to drum up enough cash to buy three of her latest paintings. *Alors*, I knocked on a door, and three little kids piled out to see the *étranger*. This was the right house! Maël is the oldest at six, Corentin is in the middle around three, and Lucile is the baby at almost two. I never realized how energetic youngsters can be until I saw Arnaud, who's three, and these children. It's like they've been drinking that precious black stuff.

The hot and cold Brittany weather had gotten to me—I started to lose my voice, and my throat was a mess. We played with the kids, ate lunch, and napped a while until Cécile came to take me to the art gallery that represents her work. Here we go again—yes, I bought a beautiful painting by a local artist named Verger, who paints with lots of royal blue and bright yellow. It would cost three hundred dollars just to send it home to Wilmington. Two of Cécile's Van Gogh-like paintings will accompany the larger one after the show ends on *le 30 juin*. She has such a beautiful relaxed way with colors and forms. *Heuresement*, this time I didn't have to come up with the cash as they trusted me to wire the money directly from my bank account as soon as I returned home. *Très bien*! To begin celebrating, even though I was really sick, we had tea at a cute little tea room in the *centre ville* (downtown). When we got home, there was a party in progress, so I tried to enjoy myself. Yet talking was doubly difficult, because even a nasal language like French requires a strong and healthy throat. Cécile's husband, Laurent, offered everyone his or her choice of *cider*, *bière*, *muscat* wine, whisky, or fruit juice and chips. Since my friends had just returned

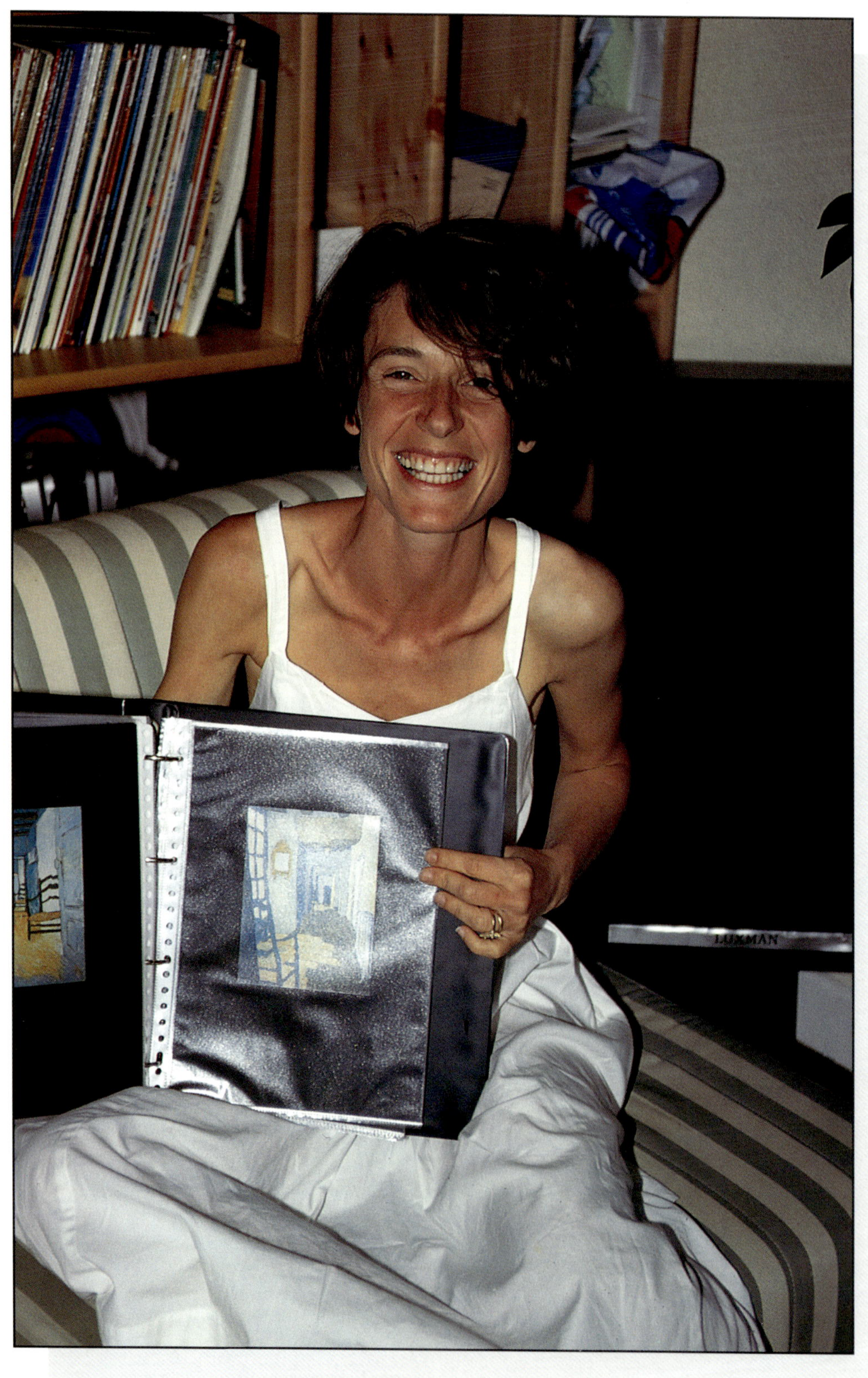

Cécile with a photo of one of her paintings which appears on the back cover of this book.

from Greece, we dined on Greek salad, cold meats, cheeses, lots of wine, and cassis, lime, and rum raisin *glace* (ice cream). One of the guests brought out a bottle of forty-year-old *eau de vie* (strong brandy), which we poured into a glass and lit on fire. We melted sugar cubes in the flame until the glass was full of *caramel* (burnt sugar). The lights were out and while the sugar melted a beautiful blue flame appeared. *Chouette* (So cool)! Then everyone drank spoonfuls of the sweeter and tamer nectar of life. *Pas mal comme truc*! (Not bad at all!)

Nantes, dimanche 4 juin

Nantes, Sunday, June 4th

Malade (sick)!

Until a breakfast of toast and that precious black fuel, I was a zombie. Once the blood was flowing again, I shared some of my *jeu de mots* (word games) with my friends, like, "*Monet n'avait pas beaucoup de monnaie, alors, pour* 10 *francs il a peint mon nez, pas* Monet, *vous comprenez*?" *Monnaie* and *mon nez* are pronounced just like *Monet*. ("Monet didn't have a lot of money [*monnaie*], but for 10 francs, he painted my nose [*mon nez*], not Monet, understand [*comprenez*]?")

We watched a little of the Roland Garros Tennis Tournament, a very popular nationwide event that is ten times more publicized than the American equivalent in Flushing Meadows. Why? Because the French are *fiers*. Yes, they are proud, and the whole country seems to come together for a common purpose every time there is an election, a holiday, a crisis, *une fête de la musique* (festival of music), or a sporting event. America rarely if ever unites in a common cause except for something like Desert Storm.

Cécile showed me a photograph of her painting called "*Le Village du Pecheur*" ("The Fishing Village"), and I had to have it, but it was at a gallery one hour away. She called the gallery, only to discover that the work had been sold one hour earlier. *Tant pis pour moi* (Too bad for me)! *C'est la vie*! Friends and relatives came over early for the evening, *alors*, we all took a delightful walk through the *Jardin des Plantes*, which is a beautiful park with a walking path that peacefully ovals around what the French call a garden. I started to feel dizzy, so Laurent and I walked back and I took a nap until Mom called. She must have sensed that I was sick; it did lift my spirits. More friends arrived while we were trying to get reservations at a French restaurant on a Sunday night at 21h00. *Bonne chance*! We opted for a nearby Chinese restaurant called La Jonque, which was very good—*cocktail maison*, Peking soup, Peking duck, rice, red wine, *beignets de banane* (banana beignets), a *petit tisane* (a hot herb beverage) at home, and "beddy by."

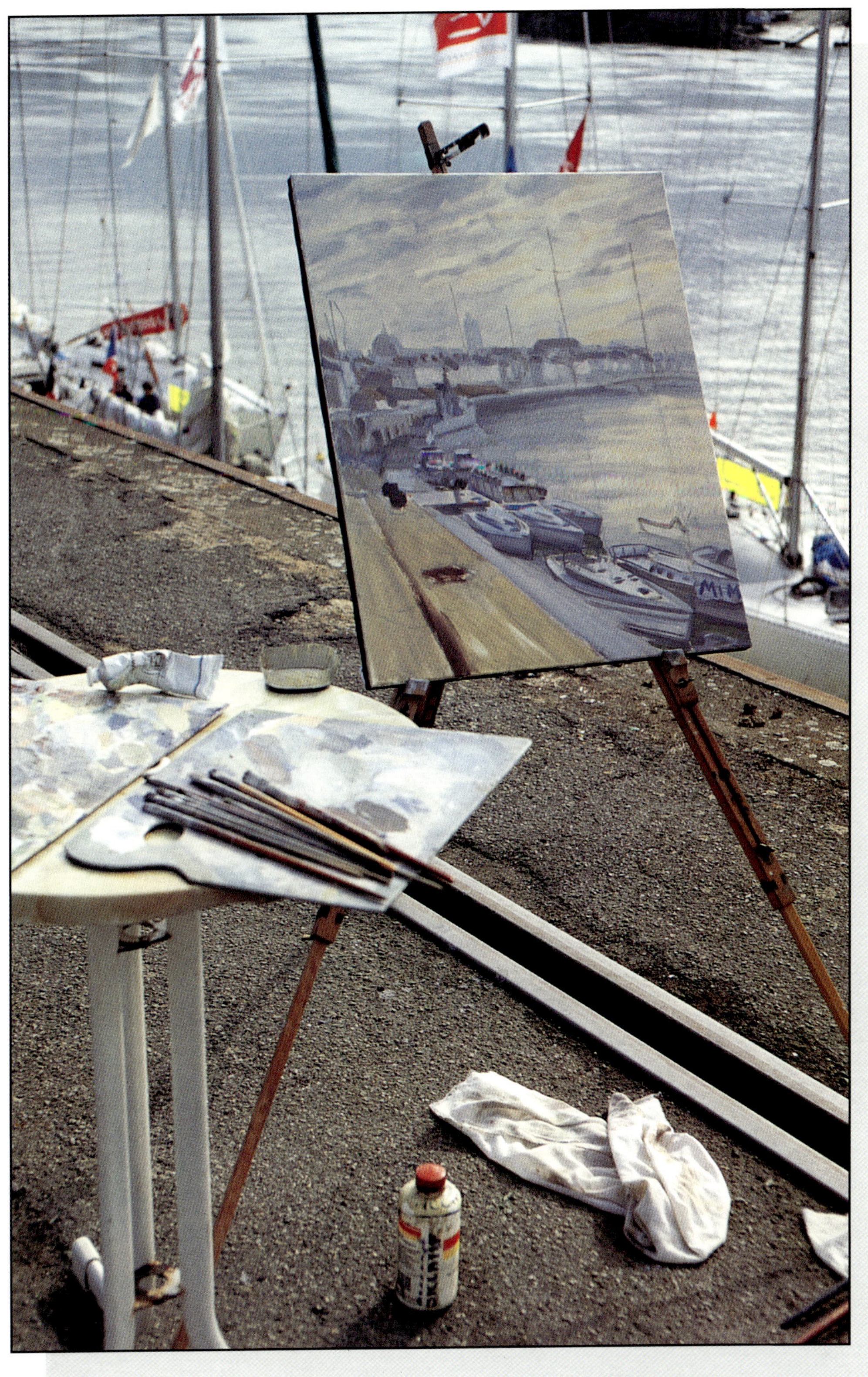

Funny how paintings often look better than the thing painted. This photo was taken at the docks of Nantes.

Vierzon, lundi 5 juin

Vierzon, Monday, June 5th

Another holiday in France! Pentecost! Everything's closed. *Merde*! Fortunately though, my friends are off today to enjoy a small *fête* at home. We had a barbecue of grilled *côtes de porc* (pork ribs) and *saucisses* (sausages) that Laurent tirelessly cooked over wood coals. A salad of fresh greens was served along with the meat and a variety of cheeses. I provided a bottle of *vin rouge*, the bottle Jacques had specifically given to me to drink in the United States. Oops!

Everyone was *au courant* (familiar) about my interest in *crêpes, alors*, Frederick and I made some for dessert. Once you have made all your French pancakes, the trick is to create a delicious hot chocolate sauce by microwaving forty percent cacao bars and milk. Leave it to the French to do difficult things in the kitchen the simple way. We sat down outside and passed around the *crêpes*, the rum raisin ice cream, and the sauce. *Quel succès* (What a success)! They were yummy, but I had to photograph the whole thing, so I wolfed down my two *crêpes* in a flash.

Time is not the same in France as it is in America or Germany. Here, no one thinks twice about being thirty minutes late; time is relative, as it is in the southern U.S. I had planned my departure, being the monochronic American that I am, for 14h00, yet it was already 16h00. I was becoming a true Francophile, and I really liked it.

When I finally tore myself away from the party, Fred and Laurent accompanied me to a gas station and then showed me the direction to Tours. The autoroute was clear, and in no time I was driving around Tours to get pointed in the direction of Vichy.

Believe it or not, "Billy" is a French name, and so far I have found two villages in France named "Billy," one near Vichy, and this one near Vierzon. *C'est très drôle* (It's very funny)!

The sun was setting upon the rail yard of Vierzon, *so* I quickly parked and trotted down to the bridge to capture the mood. I hadn't noticed it until I was about to leave, but I was in a rough-looking part of town. Luckily, "rough-looking" in France is not the same thing as "rough-looking" in the U.S. In America, I

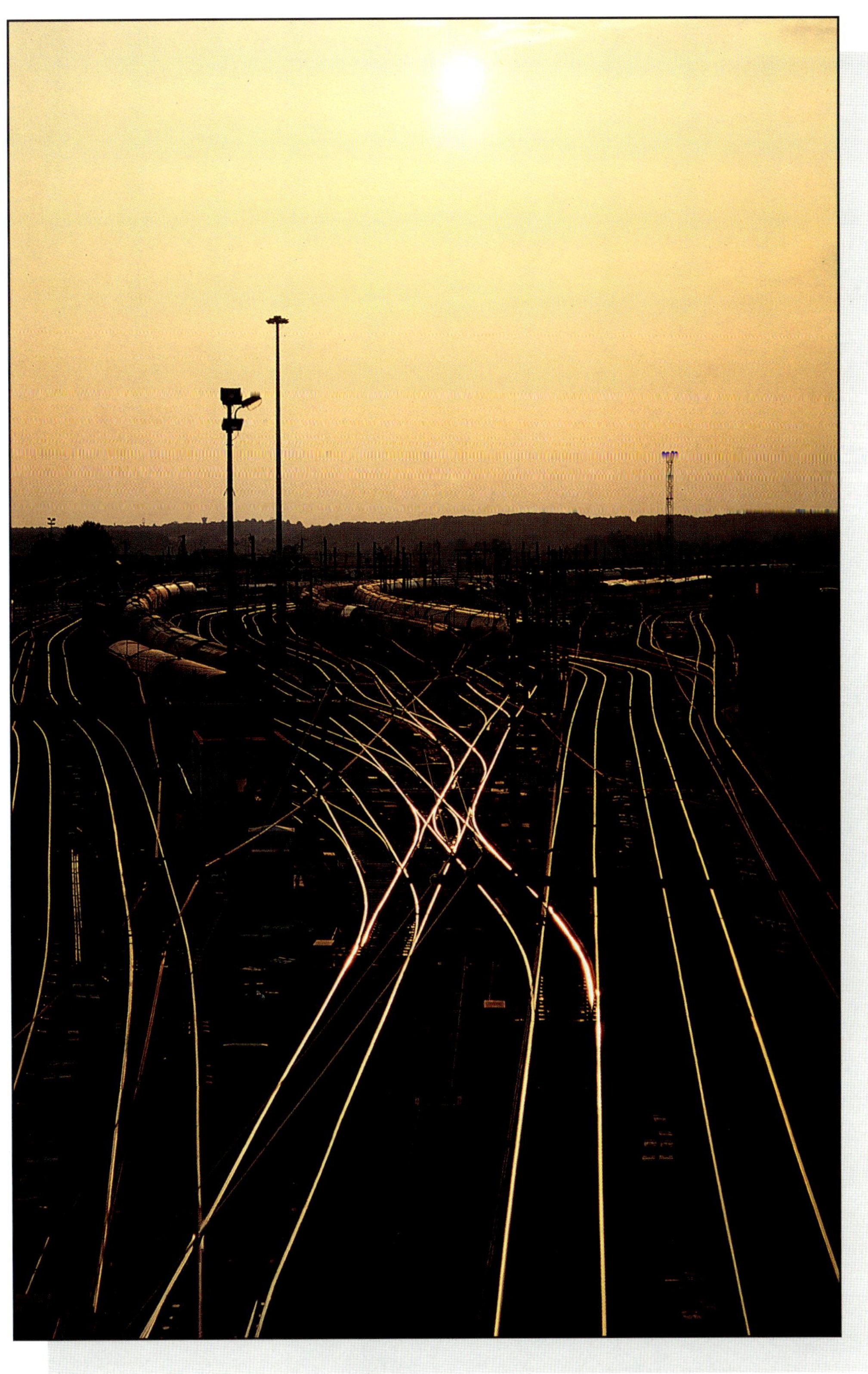

Sunset over the tracks at the Vierzon station.

probably would have been robbed, beaten, or possibly killed. Another *grande différence* between the *deux pays* (two countries)!

The Campanile Motel, a chain similar to Howard Johnsons with decent restaurants, was several miles away and open on this holiday, unlike some other hotels in town. Although I was sick, I still had my appetite, and the restaurant had a salad bar, a small food bar, lots of cheeses to choose from, and desserts. Was I dreaming? This was an American sort of thing. This was health food, and very reasonably priced. I skipped the cheese, but did much damage to *les crudités* (raw vegetables), which are so tasty in France. After dinner my brother Steve called me back from the States, and we caught up a bit. *Bons rêves*!

Vichy, mardi 6 juin

Vichy, Tuesday, June 6th

Driving along on my way to Vichy, my cheap rental car tape player ate my Pink Floyd tape. *Merde* again! *Heureusement*, I got all of the loose tape out, but I wouldn't tempt fate right away until I had cleaned the heads with cleaner from LeClerc in Vichy. At one point I was driving 160 *kilometers heure* (about 100 MPH), and getting passed, besides, that's all the "little red wagon" could do downhill.

Once I had arrived, I ate a salad at a popular lunch spot and then called Madame Bonnefoy, my *"mère francaise"* ("French mother"). "*Dring, dring, dring. Allo! Madame Bonnefoy, c'est Billy. Oui, Billy. Ça va? Ça va bien, mais où êtes-vous? Ici à Vichy. Oui, Vichy.*" Turns out that she had just readied "my room" in the basement that morning, even though she had no warning that I was coming. *Quelle chance* (what luck)! She wanted to take a nap while I did my laundry in town, and I was to come by *plus tard* (later). How perfect! When I arrived, Madame greeted me and prepared some afternoon tea and biscuits so we could relax and catch up on things. She spent much of the winter in Spain as usual, returning to Vichy mainly to take care of students from CAVILAM. This older woman is a *sainte*, and, boy, can she cook. I gain weight every time I stay with her, but I'm not complaining. We always have these serious discussions about my life and what I should be doing about it. At a certain point of seriousness I give up and go watch television. Every morning she is up early to fix breakfast and clean the house until it's spotless. Seems like she's always working at something. Her citroën is as old as I am, and believe it or not, she still drives it often to town and back.

Still feeling punk, I rested in my room until close to dinner, at which time I called my first-ever teacher in France, who had asked me over to have dinner that evening. Turns out that my friend, Anny, wasn't feeling well either, so Madame invited me to join her and the Norwegian woman who was also a short term *locataire chez* (boarder at the home of) Madame Bonnefoy. We dined on a roasted potato omelette with chives, a green salad with lots of fresh garlic, and red wine. After the excellent meal, we watched a little Dirty Harry, of all things, and I hit the sack. I couldn't sleep all night, my throat was killing me, and I was a bit worried that I would have to be treated by a *médecin étranger* (foreign doctor). A *demain, j'espère*! (See you tomorrow, I hope!)

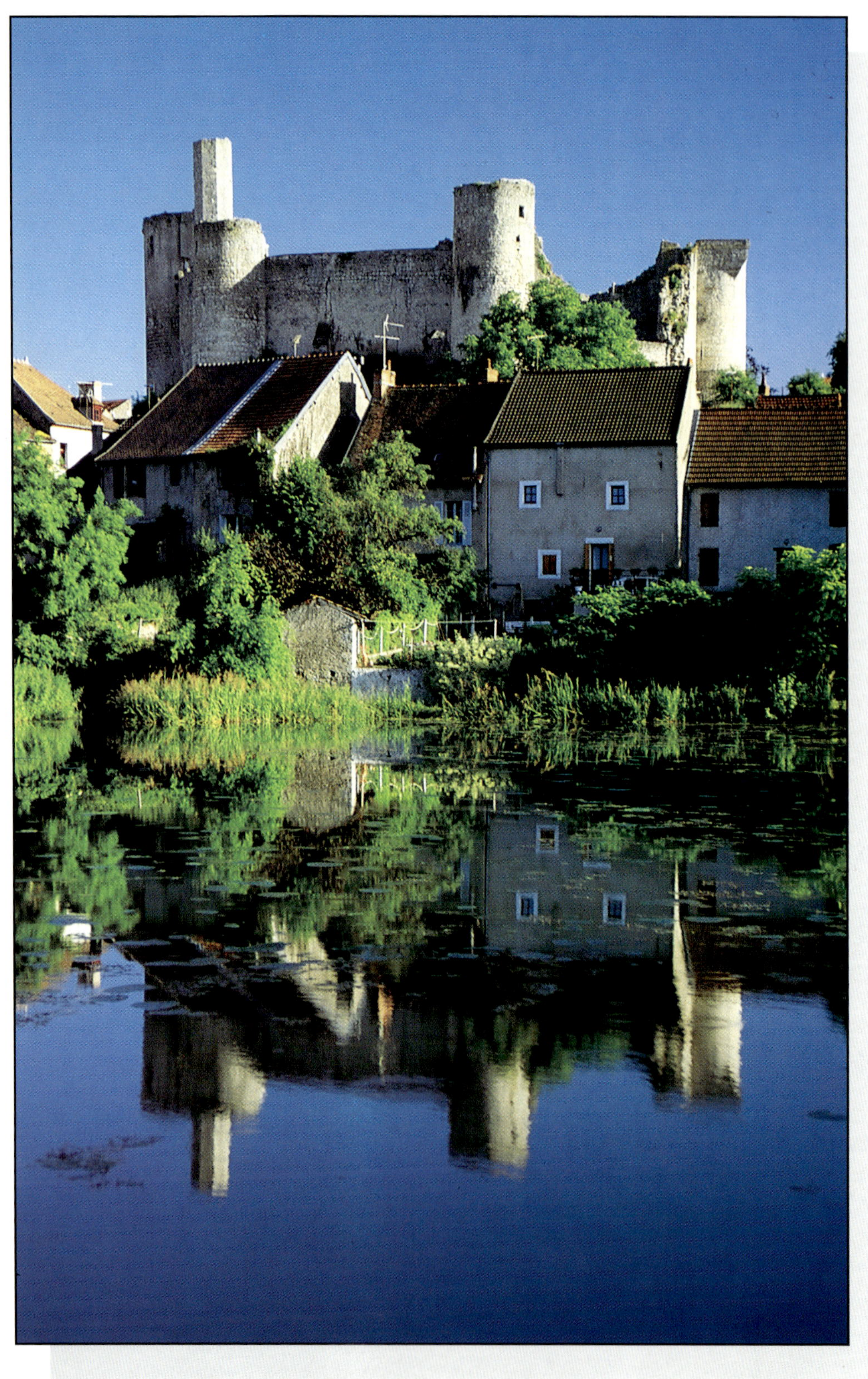

The village of Billy with the ruins of the Chateau de Billy in the background.

Vichy, mercredi 7 juin

Vichy, Wednesday, June 7th

Dizzy, headachy, and just feeling miserable, I called and got an appointment with Madame's doctor. I figured that all I needed was antibiotics, but the doctor looked at my throat and prescribed something for inflammation, something for bronchitis (an inhaler), something for my terrible coughing at night (a thick, sweet, orange-flavored syrup that tasted better than candy), and lastly, and most importantly, an antibiotic that dissolves in water and tastes bad. No wonder the French live longer lives than most other nationalities! With all that care, who wouldn't heal and be well?

I met my friend Evelyne for a cup of hot chocolate, and I explained to her that I was looking for *une femme française* (a French wife). Suddenly, she took a keener interest in me, because at that moment I think she realized just how much I loved her country. Unfortunately, we both had to leave. I headed for *La Poste*, bought some *timbres*, mailed my *cartes postales*, and went home to lay down.

Comme d'habitude (as usual), dinner was simple yet *délicieux*—cold turkey breast, potatoes and English peas with cognac and cream, *salade verte* (green salad), cheeses, and strawberries in wine, water, and sugar. *Très bon*! *Après le dîner* (after dinner), I drove to a nearby phone booth and the throttle stuck on the "little red wagon." I thought the engine was going to explode. It didn't, and I managed to drive for short distances until I was parked in front of the house again. *Quelle histoire* (What a mess)! So I called SODEXA Assistance in Paris, and they sent a *depanneur* (repairman), whose shop was thirty kilometers away. They came and let us know, in not-so-subtle a manner, that they were not happy about the long drive at night, obviously trying to lay a guilt trip on us. The older man fooled with the throttle, started the car, went around the block, and said it was fixed. I believed him and felt reassured, but by that time Madame had about had it with all of the day's excitement. "*Je regrette de vous avoir derangé aujourd'hui*" (Sorry to have bothered you today), was all I could say before I descended the stairs to call it a day.

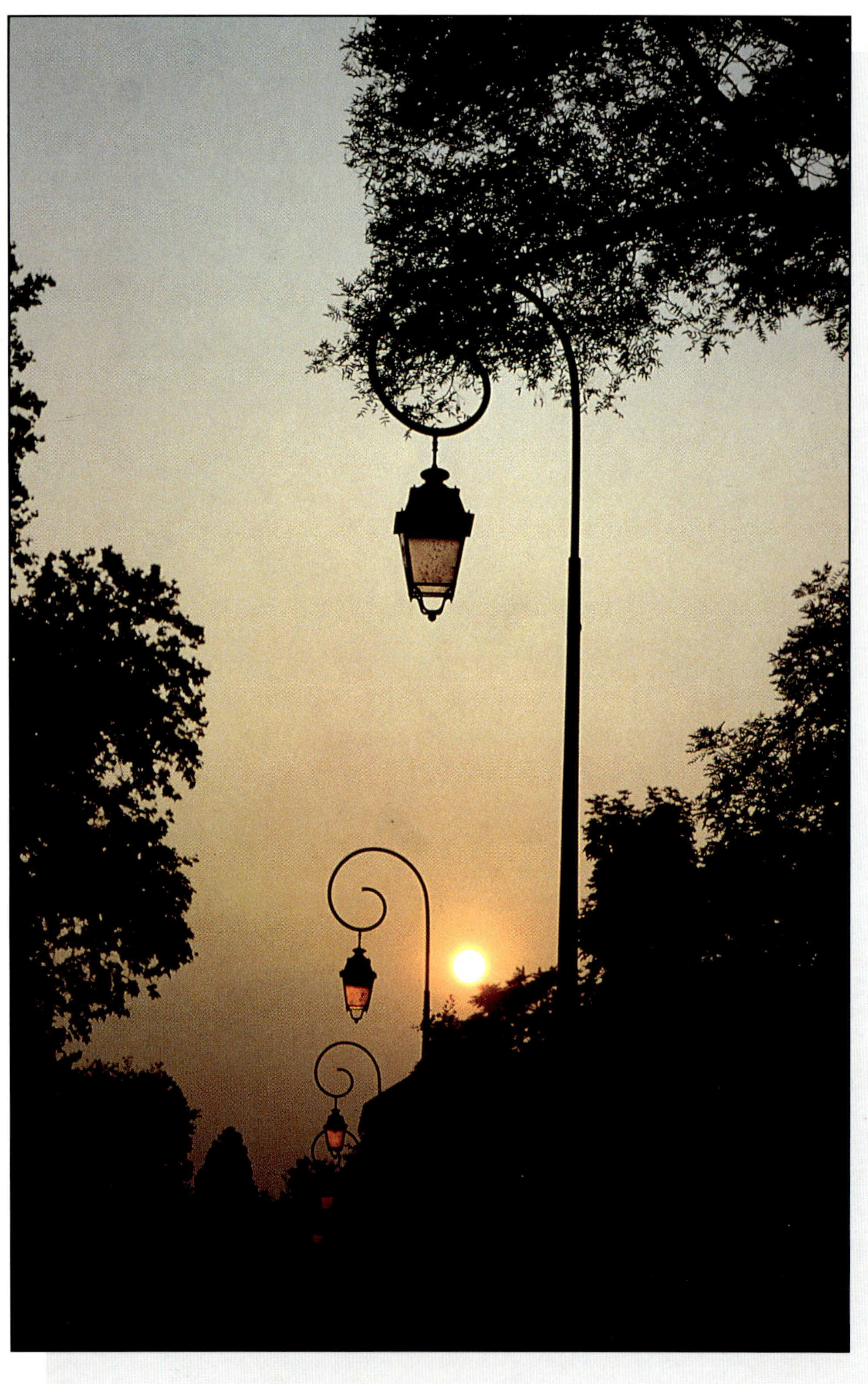

Looking down the Avenue de France in Vichy at the street lamps in the falling sun.

Vichy, jeudi 8 juin

Vichy, Thursday, June 8th

La voiture était encore en panne (The car was still broken down)! Yes, the throttle continued to stick on the little Peugeot, so I decided to walk everywhere that day and worry later. Around 11h00 Evelyne dropped by to visit, and Madame B. and the two of us talked about Spain and other vacation destinations (this is what French people like most to talk about—*les vacances*), until Evelyne suggested she and I take a walk in the park. She had just finished writing her second book, called *Cusset Pas À Pas* (*Cusset Step By Step*). It's all about the history of Vichy's little sister village. I really admire anyone who can actually write a book and see it through to publication and distribution. We said good-bye, and I hurried to meet Anny at L'Autre Source, the only local *bar à vin* (wine bar). They specialize in *Poilâne* bread *tartines*, which are basically toast or grilled bread with all kinds of delicious things spread or placed on top. Mine had garlic spread, parma ham, and Saint-Nectaire cheese, which came with a salad. Anny had one of garlic spread, tomatoes, and *tapenade*. Dessert was unforgettably stupendous—fresh strawberries, brown sugar, lavender, mascarpone cheese,

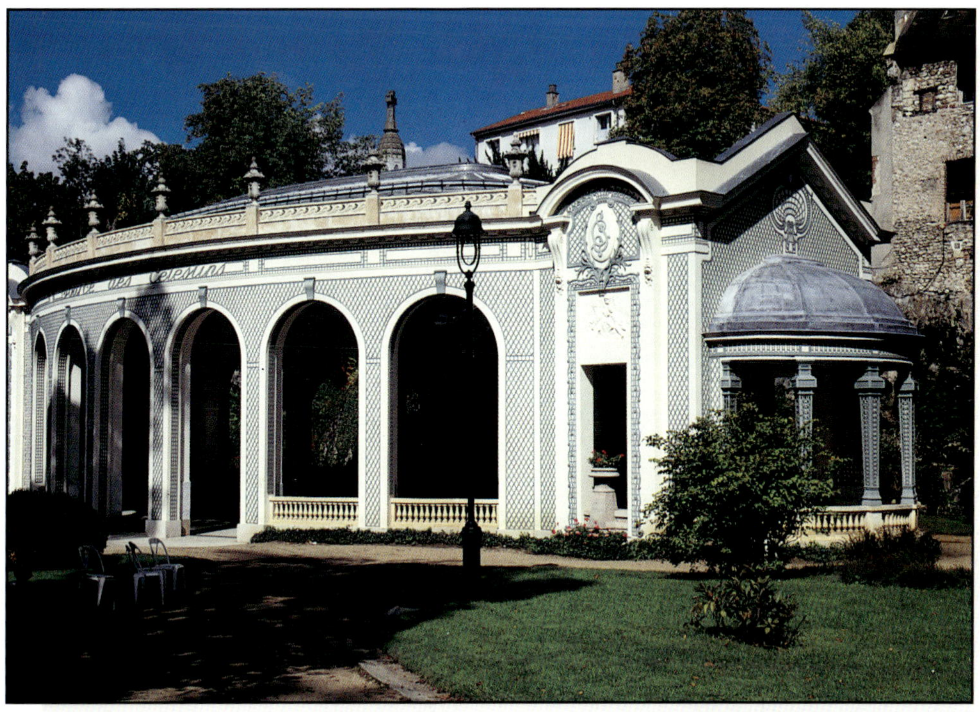

The Source des Celestins in Vichy.

and a little butter. All I can say is that often the simplest things are the most sublime. This dessert was proof.

Nap time! When I awoke, I went and changed some traveler's checks, so I could buy an awesome RAKU ram's head, or *bélier*. Although there is never a guarantee that what you buy in Europe will get to your home, you just have to go on trust as I did in this case. So far, I have always received everything I have ever sent from France. I cannot say the same for Italy.

I had tea time at a neat little *salon de thé/patisserie* called *Le Poucin Bleu* near one of the springs where elderly folks, seeking *Le Cure*, fill their plastic bottles with precious *eau de Vichy*. France has a serious problem with alcoholism and there was a time, not too long ago, when wine was safer to drink than water, not to mention cheaper than bottled waters in some cases. As you can imagine, alcohol-related diseases are also a problem, but for those who can afford it, there is "The Cure," which has been known to take a liver bombarded by fifty or sixty years of *foie gras, fromage*, and *vin rouge*, and miraculously heal it, extending the life of its owner by many years. The French believe! There are *sources* and healing centers all over the *Hexagon* (a name for and the geographical shape of France).

Tonight we had *Quiche Lorraine, salade, fromages, fromage blanc* with sugar, and a little of my kind of cure, very old grape juice. At bedtime I medicated myself and read a magazine called *Le Nouvel Observateur*, but sleep did not come easy. Once I did get to REM, I had a dream that I was making wine and speaking French with family members. How bizzare!

Orange, vendredi 9 juin

Orange, Friday, June 9th

Traveling day! Woke up early, got ready, and since the accelerator was still stuck, Madame B. called her Peugeot garage at Bellerive across the Allier river, and I improvised by playing with the clutch, turning the car on and off, and praying. After burning rubber a few times, I pulled into the tiny garage where the owner's wife wanted to know for sure that they would be reimbursed for the repairs. After several phone calls to Peugeot Central, she gave a look of satisfaction, and her husband and two other mechanics went to work. *Le monsieur* took the car for a test drive, and I was on my way again.

But they didn't fix anything, and I soon found out. *Quelle blague* (what a joke)! But no way! No more *depanneurs* until I get to Saint-Tropez. Since I drive at full throttle all the time on the autoroute anyway, I figured *pas de problème*. I wanted to stop and eat lunch, but I needed to find a place where I could watch the "little red wagon," since it was full of my camera equipment and clothes—*McDoe*! Right in front of this American success story was one parking space out of hundreds in a huge mall. *Quelle chance* (What luck)! The salmon and shrimp salad hit the spot, and I was off and throttling my way to Provence in no time.

In Orange, I checked into a room at the Campanile motel, locked my bags in the room, and walked into town with my "traveling companion." *Malheureusement*, the only thing this old city had to offer was the ancient theater built by the Romans. Later, at the buffet, I made a salad of cukes and tomatoes, mozzarella cheese, mushroom caps with little onions, and endive. No bread, no main course, but I did have dessert: dark berries in their juices, mint-flavored pear halves, kiwi, and *crème anglaise*. *C'est mon regime* (It's my diet)!

I called Alain and Janine, my last year's host family in Perpignan, to say *bonjour* and find out if they had received the bottle of Gundlach Bundschu Merlot that I sent last summer. They had, but they would not think of drinking it until I could be there to enjoy it with them. And they meant it. How wonderfully French!

Television, medications, and sleep—maybe I'll be well *demain*.

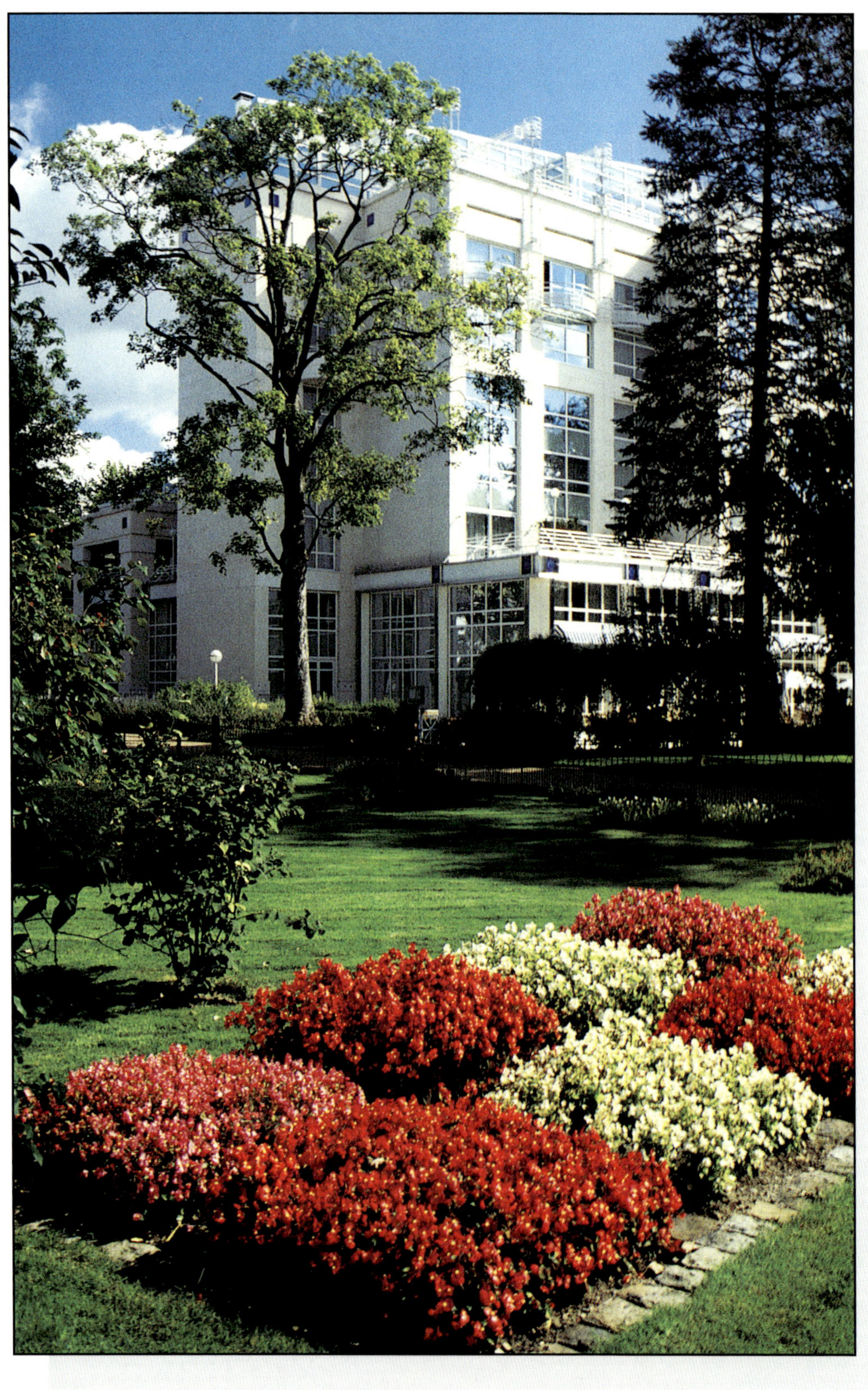

The grand Hotel des Celestins,
one of Vichy's newest and finest spas.

Saint-Tropez, samedi 10 juin

Saint-Tropez, Saturday, June 10th

Up at the crack of dawn, ritual *petit déj*, and off to the races, literally. Luckily, the autoroute was just next door. I made it to Saint-Tropez, but not before getting behind a Czechoslovakian travel bus. *Merde*! I couldn't help thinking that they are at war in their backyards, and yet life goes on, because these fortunate ones are vacationing in France. There's hope yet.

Robert, the son of the owner of the hotel, arrived at the Dëi Marres shortly after me, and we fixed ourselves a nice salad for lunch. In eleven years he hasn't changed a bit. He still looks like a young Jean-Paul Belmondo, the popular French actor. Must be all the tennis and yoga he practices, or *le soleil* (sunshine).

They put me in #7, my lucky number and a perfect room with a bathtub to soothe my muscles after working out. After the light meal, I drove into town to take some pictures of the charming yet touristy town. On my way back I bought provisions at *Prisunic*—mineral water, exotic juices, Fanta orange drink, batteries, and #4 suntan cream. *Il fait chaud* (The weather is hot)! *Alors*, I had to take a swim in the refreshing crystal clear waters of the pool, so I lubed-up and dove in. Brrr—they must refrigerate their pool here. After a short nap by the cooling tank, I cleaned up, and this time, when I tried to start "Red," the accelerator was too *coincé* (stuck) to drive it. Once again, I called Paris, and once again they sent a *depanneur* from Timbuktu. But this very friendly man *aimable* found the culprit of the recurring *problème*. He said, "*C'est simple, la manette de gaz est coincé* (It's simple. The throttle is stuck)." No joke! But this *mec* pulled the throttle wire out of the little clamp that the factory installed to hold it to the chassis, and *voilà*! Fixed! Understandably, I still had my doubts, but he assured me that he "got" the problem. *On verra*! (We'll see!)

At 20h30 I found myself sitting in a beautifully-decorated, empty restaurant on a Saturday evening, because a local suggested I dine there. The last time I trusted locals was in Avignon, and the meal and the service were outstanding despite the fact that I was their only customer that entire evening. They waited on me hand and foot as if I were some kind of king.

Here in Saint-Tropez the tourists are quite fickle, and often a mediocre restaurant will become *la mode* (popular fashion), while nearby competitors suffer. This restaurant was an example. The *resto* next door was packed with tourists, while I ate a delicious, reasonably-priced meal in tranquility, *grace à Dieu* (thank God). I had smoked *margret de canard* (sliced duck breast), salad with pine nuts and tomatoes, and *gratin d'aubergines*, which I believe I can make at home. I would make it with olive oil, diced eggplant, diced zucchini, sliced black olives, garlic, parmesan cheese, tomatoes, red peppers, onions, *du sel et du poivre* (salt and pepper), and *herbes de Provence*. *Victoire*! The car worked all the way back to the room. Maybe that *mec* was right. By the way, "*mec*" is not short for "mechanic." It's simply slang for "guy" or "dude" in French.

The Beautiful People are here. In addition to the Porsches and Mercedes, there are sleek streamlined monstrosities of the sea with twenty-four hour crews. Unreal! Tomorrow I'm invited to Robert's forty-fifth birthday party here at the Dëi Marres.

My *resto* will have display shelf space for things like chocolates, *herbes de Provence*, coffees, teas, other candies, and specialty foods, maybe even my favorite wines. At first, we will buy our breads and pastries from a real French bakery in town, later making our own. We'll have personal wine tastings every night for tables of four or more, but reservations may be required twenty-four hours in advance. Sweet dreams are made of these! *Bonne nuit*!!

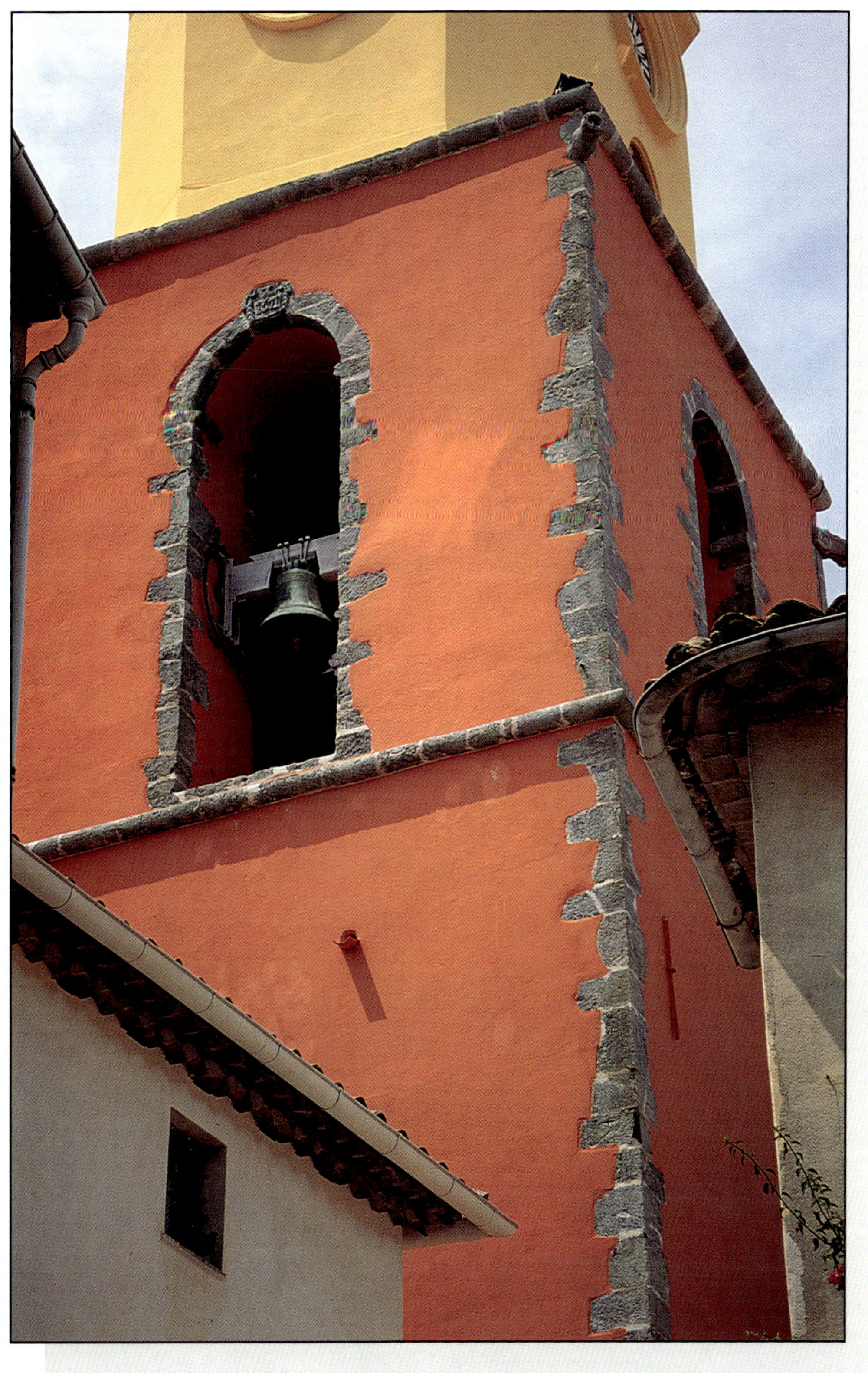

An all familiar landmark of Saint-Tropez,
the colorful bell tower.

Saint-Tropez, dimanche 11 juin

Saint-Tropez, Sunday, June 11th

Today was sunny, yet I still had to wear my sweatshirt. How can it be so cool at the Côte d'Azur in June? The heat and humidity will do me good when I get home. Every foot of this world needs an inch of North Carolina.

I continued my exploration of town with camera in hand, sunshine on my subject. At lunch I met Marc, a waiter who wants to help me with the *resto*, and his advice, well taken, was to focus on one thing and do it well before spreading myself too thin by going in ten different directions. My new friend brought me some famed *soupe de poisson* (fish soup), with spicy mayo, French bread croutons, and shredded Swiss cheese. Next, I had grilled turbot with a tarragon cream sauce and fruit salad for dessert. Despite my efforts, I cannot diet here—maybe at home, but not while in France. The food is just too tasty here.

I had a good long nap with the TV on and then got ready for some drinking. I was just having *un verre de champagne* at Robert's forty-fifth and was being totally

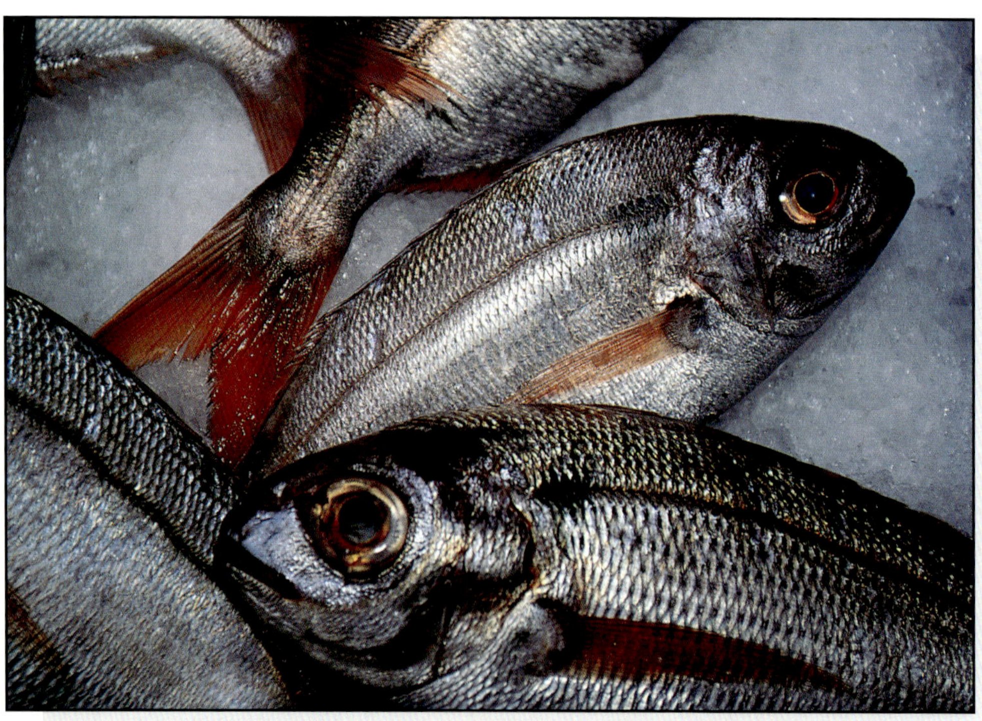

At the fish market of Saint-Tropez.

ignored (a very common occurrence for foreigners at French dinner parties), when I decided to make conversation with this woman. Boy, was she a bitch. She just made some cute remark and proceeded to ignore me. I hate the way some people can be. So uncivilized! In the world I choose to live in, people try to make others feel better about themselves, but it would be quite naive to think that my world extended much beyond my own dreams. When my friend Constance arrived I was much happier, because she's not only from my world, but she's also gorgeous. Divorced from a Frenchman since 1988, she decided to make France her permanent address. I met her and her husband in the spring of '84 when I was staying at the Dëi Marres, recovering from a paella food poisoning I had received in Grenoble. We caught up a bit, and I found myself very attracted to Constance. I went to bed thinking that I have gotten too used to being alone and having things my way and having them always go so smoothly. Seeing such a thing of beauty as I did tonight makes me think of giving up some of my freedom to have that extra someone always around with little ones playing at our sides. Gee whiz, it is bedtime.

Saint-Tropez, lundi 12 juin

Saint-Tropez, Monday, June 12th

Up early, breakfast in my room, and tennis lessons at 10h00. Robert has been teaching tennis at the club here for over fifteen years, and it is obvious that he likes what he does. After two hours in the sun, we found some shade, where he taught me a little yoga. Healthful salad for *le déjeuner* (lunch). In the afternoon I took "Red" to the Peugeot garage for a 2500 kilometer *révision* (checkup), and it struck me as typically French that the owner and his wife live above and run the operation. To me that seems to be the ultimate business arrangement, and family-run businesses seem to have the most longevity. What could be the vital ingredient?

I drove into town to mail some *cartes postales*, and came back for a nap. Around 17h30, I wound my way up to the village of Ramatuelle, where I had a field day with my camera. The light was kind of milky, with an almost magical quality. What a wonderful day! I was already thriving on the anticipation of dining with Constance, who was going to meet me at Les Terraces at the Hotel Baou.

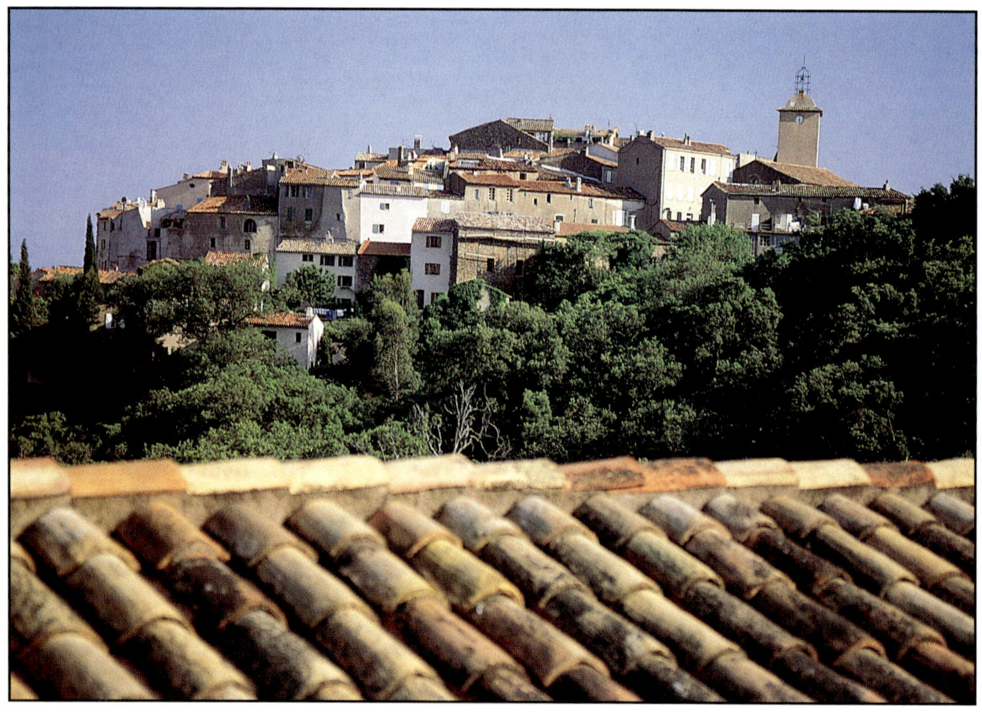

Ramatuelle from a distance.

When she entered the hotel wearing a short white dress and heels it was as if someone turned on auxiliary lighting all around us. Surely I was in the presence of an angel. Although the excellent service was very American, the food was brilliantly *français*. The waiter wanted us to see that the champagne he was pouring for our *Kir Royals* was really from the designated region in France called Champagne, otherwise it could have been any of a number of cheap sparkling wines from *n'importe où* (anywhere). We shared the sauteed *foie gras de canard* with tiny lentils on a bed of greens, and to top that, slivers of that precious black delicacy from Provence, *truffles*. Since Chateau Minuty produces and bottles wines just a matter of miles from here, we opted for a bottle of their red and were not disappointed. For the main course we had *saumon à la barigoule* (a delicious filet of salmon grilled and then finished with mushrooms, garlic, ham, and onions), a zucchini mousse, and those white things that look like potatoes but taste like radishes. Dessert was pear halves on *pain perdu*, which is the original french toast, with crystallized ginger and caramel ice cream. *C'était très bon* (It was delicious)!

From our vantage point we could see the full moon rise up over the Mediterranean into the clear southern sky, beaming to overpower the light of the stars around it. Talk about romantic! Constance showed me around her flat and offered me an after-dinner drink. I chose the *"trou Normande,"* or Calvados, a very strong apple brandy that makes a *"trou"* ("hole") in your stomach so you don't feel so full. She sipped on some Grand Marnier, and we sat together on her leather sofa talking in *franglais* (a combination of French and English words), laughing about the similarities of our failed marriages, and getting under the influence. Just as I moved a little closer to Constance, the conversation changed to sex, but I think that's when my pen ran out of ink, and I unfortunately had a short bout of amnesia. *Bonne nuit! A demain!*

Saint-Tropez, mardi 13 juin

Saint-Tropez, Tuesday, June 13th

She looked so childlike, lying there in her bed asleep, so I kissed her cheek and left the note on the night stand. Tennis was better today than yesterday, and I really got into the yoga breathing exercises *à la Robert*. We both had lunch at the tennis club down the street—salad, omelette with cheese and chives, and *pommes frites* (French fries).

At 15h00, after a nap, I met Marc at the restaurant where he works, and we went to the Crêperie Bretonne to talk about *crêperies*, naturally. I had one with chocolate and vanilla ice cream and Grand Marnier, which reminded me of that first kiss the night before; I'm daydreaming! The restaurant had a very small kitchen right in the middle as you walk in with eight to ten *plaques* to cook on. All *crêpes* are made when ordered, not like those soggy things you sometimes get on the street in Paris, so when it's crowded the pressure is on. Things can get pretty hectic in a place like the Bretonne. I need to visit *crêperies* in the U.S. to see how they operate. I'll call the chambers of commerce of Saint Louis,

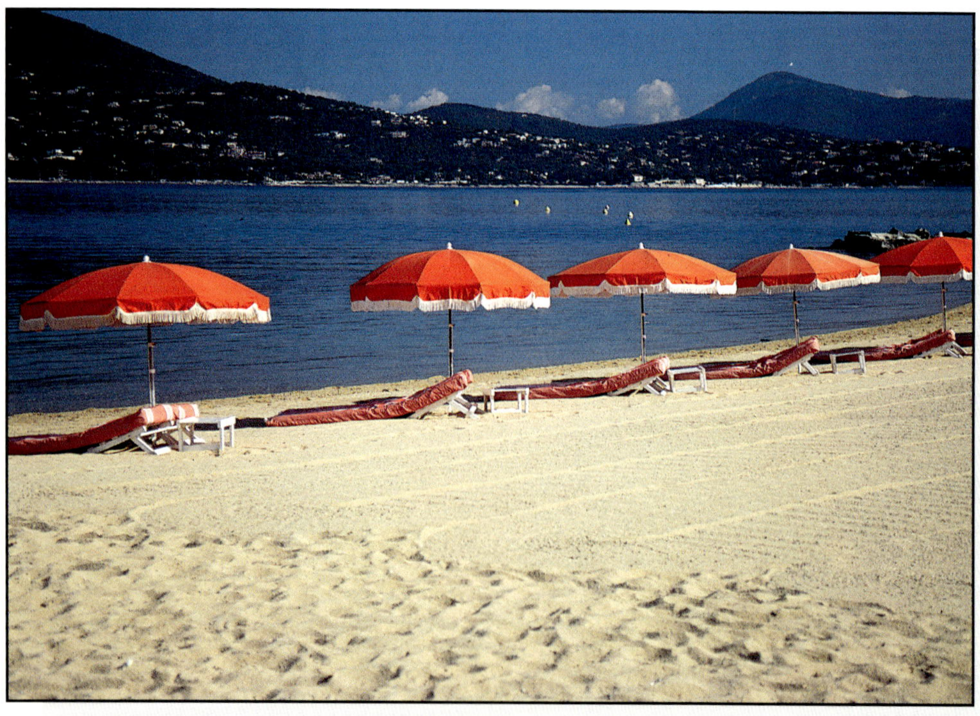

Umbrellas along the bay at Saint-Tropez.

Chicago, Houston, and San Francisco. Since Marc used to work there, the owner comped our *crêpes*. See, the French really are extremely friendly and hospitable people.

We then went by Marc's flat, really a small room with beautiful views of the sea on one side and of the forest on the other. I left and was feeling a little weak, so I read in my room until it was time to bathe and go back to the very same *crêperie* for dinner. The "special" which I ordered was onions, bacon, and egg, but that didn't really send me. Oh well! Next, I ate my second sweet *crêpe* of the day with ice cream and Grand Marnier.

The customary beverage to consume with French pancakes is *cidre bouché*, and their Val de Rance sparkling apple cider, at 2% alcohol, was excellent. After four cups I didn't feel a thing, meaning I didn't even have a buzz. I'll have to order some of those coffee cups they use to drink cider from for my *crêperie* back home.

Constance was home, and we talked for about an hour before hitting the sack. She's pretty awesome. Tomorrow we all were going to a nudist beach. Can't wait!

Saint-Tropez, mercredi 14 juin

Saint-Tropez, Wednesday, June 14th

Still feeling a little rough—they brought hot coffee and croissants with an assortment of homemade jams to give me *la force* (strength) to play tennis until noon. I was even better today than the day before.

Marc and Constance met me at the club for lunch, and I could feel my heart racing with her near. What had happened to me? I felt like a kid. It was obvious that Marc was impressed with my date, because he almost spilt the B*adoit* on her plate he was so nervous. After the light meal, I followed Marc's directions on how to get to *la plage naturiste* (the nudist beach). The road had a lot of curves, so it seemed like a long way, but it was actually close to Saint-Trop as the crow flies. A*lors*, once we found a parking space we walked along the cliffs and around bolders for what also seemed like a long way, but I was just in a hurry to see if Marc was telling the truth.

E*t oui*! There they were. Mostly naked men but some women as well. What a disappointment! I mean, after you've pierced the veil of mystery and actually seen a *naturiste* beach, it's no big deal. Me? No way! I kept my manhood a secret and so did Marc, but to our utter amazement, Constance, who was catching rays on her back with her top undone, turned over. Wow! I could almost hear Marc gulp as my own precious machine fluttered. How can I describe such perfection in construction? I guess I can't here, but all I can say is, I take back everything I said about nude beaches. They are a place of beauty and intrigue, not to mention romance. And Constance is an American! I thought only the French took their tops off. Marc suggested we take a dip in the Mediterranean, and it was as if we had never seen such a sight in our lives.

We left a little while later, and my friends took off, Marc for work, Constance for home. After a thirty-minute nap, I went to town for dinner at the "crowded restaurant" of the night before, and it was terrible pseudo-Italian crap. Never trust a tourist! N*ormalement*, trust the locals!

I watched television until there was a knock on my door. It was Constance. I let her in, and we talked and watched "Starsky and Hutch" in French until the wee hours of the morning. T*rès bonne nuit*!! A *demain*!

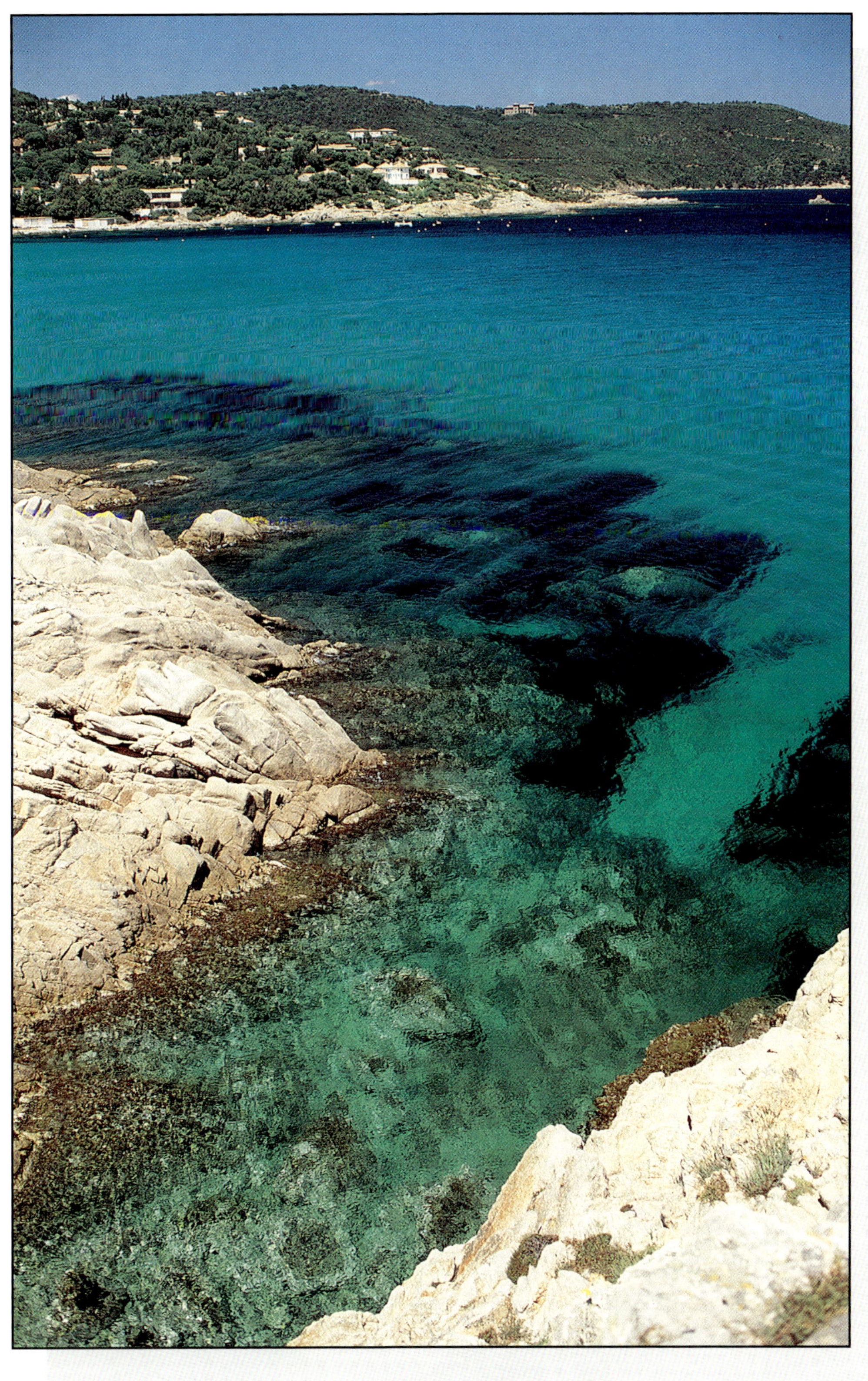

The clear waters of the Mediterranean near the nude beach.

Saint-Tropez, jeudi 15 juin

Saint-Tropez, Thursday, June 15th

Ditto as *hier matin* (yesterday morning). Lunch at the club was quite tasty—tomatoes and mozzarella, grilled filet of sole, and nougat ice cream for dessert. *Très bon*!

Today was the day we all were going to *faire de la planche à voile* (go wind surfing). We'd been planning it since my arrival, so Robert drove Beattrice, Constance, and me to the rental place by the bay, where we paid and prepped for sailing the giant surfboards. The breeze blew us away from shore, and we sailed to and fro, parallel to the shore. In other words, we were kind of stuck in that pattern until the wind changed directions or until someone brought us the centerboards we were supposed to have already. Once all three of us were out in the bay, we realized that there wasn't any more wind. After about an hour of waiting (we had only paid for one hour), we were rescued by the motor boat one by one. First Constance, then me; by that time the wind started blowing from a favorable direction, and Robert looked as if he could make it to shore.

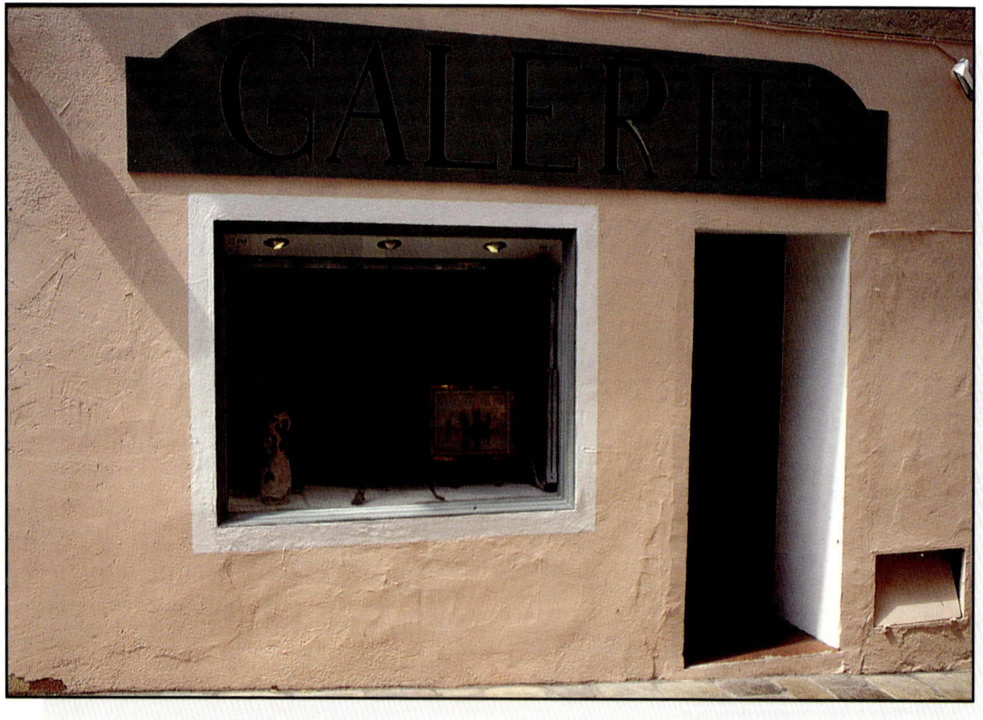

One of the many quaint shops in the town of Saint-Tropez.

He tacked and we waited until he made it all the way in. *Pas mal* (not bad) for a beginner!

Back at the hotel we all dove into the pool to wash the sand and salt from our bodies. (It's OK, Robert owns the place.) Then we drank my bottle of white burgundy *grace à* Jacques (thanks to Jack) of Lorient, and ate a cake that someone had made for Robert.

At 20h00, I picked Constance up, and we had dinner at *La Ferme* (The Farm) under a tent with plants everywhere. She had the lobster salad and the duck while I had the smoked salmon made right there and the rotisserie free-range chicken. The *sommelier* (cellarman) suggested a white, but I told him that we prefer red even with "fruits of the sea" or poultry like duck and chicken. He gave me a strange look and said in his sort of English, "Vell vat do you vent zen?" One of those bad apples! We just laughed when he left. I ordered a bottle of Chateau de Pez, a *grand vin* (great wine) from the Saint-Estephe region of Bordeaux, and we loved it with our "delicate" meal.

Constance and I are pretty much in agreement about the French and this country. We love the language, the culture, the history, the food, and the people, but every once in a while a rotten apple will come along and we find ourselves French bashing. Mind you, we're only talking about a small *pourcentage de la population*, but that small *pourcentage* is famous worldwide. Ultimately, France is no worse than any other country. We stopped ourselves and returned to a better conversation about why we love Provence so much, with its gorgeous colors, rustic splendor, seasonal warmth and tranquility, and eternal spirit.

For dessert we had Poire Belle Hélène, which is vanilla ice cream, pears, toasted almonds, hot chocolate sauce, and *chantilly*. Wow! *Mon amie* invited me over for a nightcap, and the rest is history.

Saint-Tropez, vendredi 16 juin

Saint-Tropez, Friday, June 16th

I finally beat my instructor today 6-2, and I learned a lot of *gros mots* (curse words), out of the anger of someone's discontent. However, Robert got his revenge in the next set by defeating me 6-something, but by that time I was still reeling from my first victory of the week. My improvement during these five days was consistent, and I was *heureux* (happy) to have finished with *une victoire*.

Something that happens to Anglophones and maybe to other foreigners when they immerse themselves in French is that when they begin to write in English again, some words look funny, and some are hard to spell. For example "enough" looks totally weird to me, and the French spell *département* like that. "Address" in French has one "d" and an "e" on the end. So although there are many words that are spelled identically in the two languages, many nuances still exist to trip you. "A*quisition*" has a "c" in English, and "apartment" has another "p" and an "e" after the "t" in French, and the list goes on and on.

Today I've been thinking that a *bar à vin* would be better than a *crêperie* for many reasons. One, we would have more freedom in what to serve. Two, there would be simpler logistics of getting the food out (in France, *crêperies* bring your food when it's ready, regardless of whether the other folks at the table have been served). Three, *crêperies* shoot for quantity in order to make a *franc*, while the wine bar would aim for the highest quality in food and beverage. Four, people are learning about and drinking more wine than ever before. Five, we would be getting away from the *faux* pancake stigma attached to *crêpes*. And six, and lastly, my restaurant can always serve *crêpes* as well as traditional wine bar food.

We'll always serve desserts worth saving room for, and it will not be unusual for people to order very light and then have a decadent sweet afterwards. This is not to be confused with the popular American diet—eat like a bird, drink diet soft drinks, and then consume massive quanties of some sweet, frozen, and tasteless mass of American marketing—those little powder doughnuts that people like to eat entire boxes of and would kill for, for example. S*erieusement* (Seriously), we would serve smoked Scotch salmon on buttered toast, N*ems* or Spring Rolls with mint, lettuce, and vinaigrette, tomatoes and mozzarella and basil, delicious *potages du jour* (soup of the day), Caesar, *niçoise*, and Spinach salads, *et cétera*.

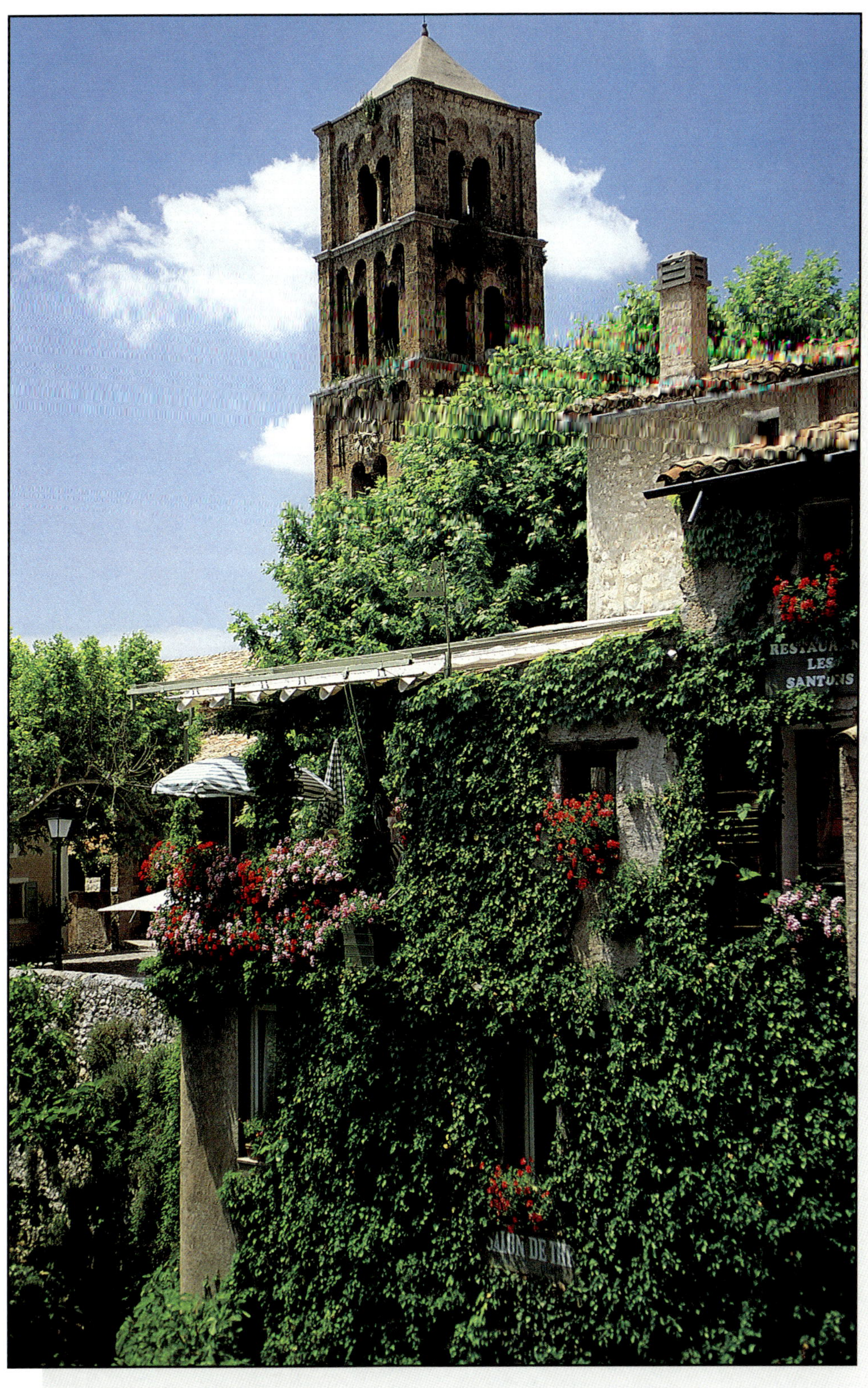

Moustiers Saint-Marie.

By the way, for lunch I had Nems and baby scallops in a saffron cream sauce. In town, I called Constance with a trusty *carte téléphonique*, and we made plans for dinner, Le Baou Terrace again. *Et oui!* As before, our dinners were scrumptious, and the service consistent. I had tiny onions in a creamy tomato *coulis* with truffles, and Constance had *carpaccio*, which is red raw beef, with olive oil and seasonings, a favorite among Parisians. Our main course was lightly battered and sauteed calamari that looked like small onion rings but tasted heavenly. Chateau Minuty red was once again the beverage of choice, and we also drank Badoit, my favorite mineral water. The *crème brulée* was *exceptionelle* and came with a *sorbet au romarin* (rosemary sherbet). Unreal!

When we parked outside her flat, she looked at me with her sparkling blue eyes and told me that the week had been the most wondrous time she had ever spent. I felt the same way too. We went inside for a dreamy night of very little sleep. *C'est l'amour! Dors biens mon choux* (Sleep well my little cabbage)! A *demain*!

Moustiers Saint-Marie, samedi 17 juin

Moustiers Saint-Marie, Saturday, June 17th

The road to Moustiers Saint-Marie was long and winding and so hot you could have fried an *œuf* on it. This was Provence in June, where the nights are often cool, but the days can be exceptionally *chaud*. After slowing down to ask another driver directions and getting good ones, I proceeded through the city mazes of twists and turns and the steep stretches of the Basse Alps until I arrived at a cute little village that looked like it was attached to the hills behind it. The *gendarme* (and I presume there was only one in such a *bled*) gave me directions on how to find La Bastide de Moustiers, and I was there in a matter of minutes.

An attractive young lady dressed in chef's clothing came over to greet me and take my bags, but I protested. She grabbed the heaviest one and said it would be *dans ma chambre* (in my room). Who was this person? I thought she was just hanging out there. But it turned out that Sonja, an attractive and mature twenty-three-year old from Sweden, was hand picked by Alain Ducasse, the world-famous French chef of the restaurant Louis XV in Monaco, to be the head chef at Ducasse's latest culinary endeavor. But La Bastide is not just about food. It is a seventeenth-century two-story potter's house with seven uniquely decorated guest rooms each appointed with a special Provençal color scheme according to its name. My room, "Lavande," was mostly blue and white and intimately comfortable.

Lunch was a salad with rabbit in a creamy brown sauce on toast, all sorts of vegetables *confits*—meaning reduced in white chicken stock, olive oil, *du sel et du poivre* (salt and pepper)—including onions, carrots, radishes, artichokes, steamed lettuce, veal stock, a slice of thick crunchy bacon, and cold creamy *brebis* (sheep's cheese) on top. The honey ice cream was delicious, especially with the red fruit *gratin* it came with. As I was heading back to town to explore and take pictures, Sonja told me that I could have the same dinner as they served for lunch or anything I wanted. Anything? I preordered the same delectable vegetable dish and my own idea, a roasted garlic salad, and left with my mouth watering again.

Since dinner is served quite late (between 20h00 and 21h00) at least in the summer, I decided to make the perilous drive to Point Sublime, about twenty-five curvy kilometers away. Like the bold fool that I can be when I have a camera in my hand, I stopped in the middle of the road (there were no shoulders) and began photographing this bull with a bell, which seemed harmless enough

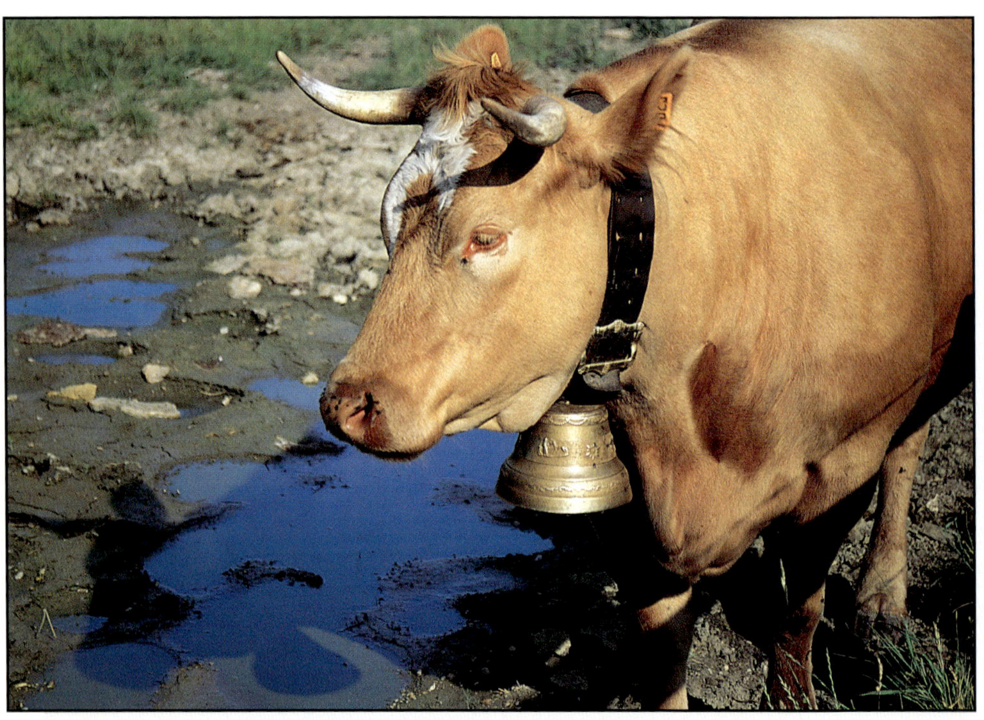

You can ring my bell.

inside the fence. After several frames, I heard a car coming, and so I rushed to get out of there as fast as I possibly could. Just as I began to pick up speed, a black monster of a Mercedes came up on my tail and laid on the horn. At least it wasn't a train! I made it, but that whatever-he-was was on my back all the way to the Point.

Any memorable dinner comes with wine, so I ordered a bottle of Chateau La Tour de L'Eveque-Côtes de Provence. I thought of Constance and wished that she were here to share in this celebration of life with me. What was she up to? Just then they brought my salad— warm thin slivers of sauteed eggplant, zucchini, roasted peeled garlic bulbs, greens, radishes, and some kind of tuber with balsamic vinegar dressing. Truly more sublime than the Point! Then came the veggies in chicken stock with the wonderful *brebis* (sheep cheese). If I married someone who cooked like this, I could easily be a vegetarian. Dessert was the same as lunch and just as delicious. I crawled under the large cozy comforter and read *Gala* (like *People* magazine) until I could no longer hold my eyes open. A *demain*!

Moustiers Saint-Marie, dimanche 18 juin

Moustiers Saint-Marie, Sunday, June 18th

The early chill of the morn greeted me out on the terrace overlooking the valley below and had me wearing a sweatshirt—quite pleasant, actually. I had delicious, buttery sugar bread, toasted brioche, and coffee. No diet here!

As the day progressed it warmed up nicely, *alors*, I headed for the brand new, state-of-the-art pool to bronze myself and listen to the new Simple Minds cassette. No topless bathing here, although one lady from Sweden looked like she belonged in *Playboy*. Her gold one-piece clung to her brown skin like the leather on a baseball, and of course the cold water made everything glisten in the sunlight. E*t oui, c'est comme ça en France* (And yes, it's like that in France)! The Beautiful People are definitely here.

I shaved my goatee, "Van Gogg" as the French would pronounce it, because of the *chaleur* (heat) when the sun is high in the Provence heavens, and not a soul noticed, or at least no one said anything about it. Very French!

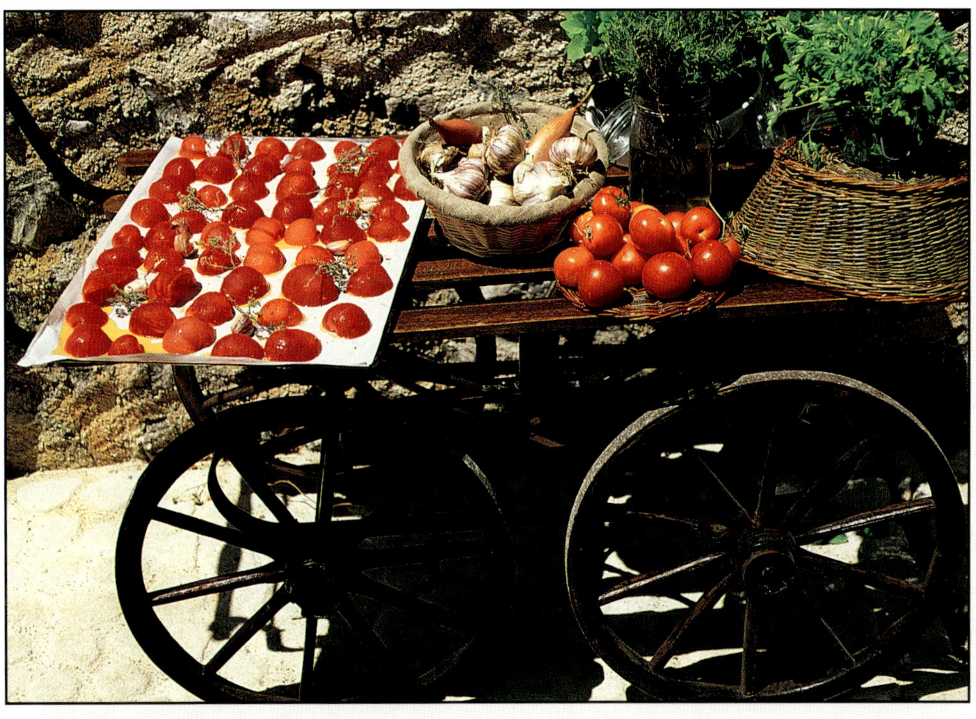

Sun drying tomatoes and other produce on an old cart outside La Bastide de Moustiers.

Someone must be watching over me. Twice, my life has been saved on this trip, and it makes me think that there is a reason why I am here; that I have unfinished business, so to speak. I hope so. Mom called, and it was great to hear her voice. Sometimes I feel like an island in the void, but rather I prefer to believe I am a small part of a great whole, and apparently right now I am needed alive in the Big Wheel, though I'll never know exactly why.

I had a chat outside with Sonja and one of her assistants while they cleaned and cut *petites* artichokes. Turns out she was going to be a dancer in the States, but that didn't work out, so she went to chef's school in Paris. Now she's a rising star working here at La Bastide for Alain Ducasse. Cooking in France, although much more delicate and flavorful, could be likened to the NBA, and top chefs are the superstars who do the commercials. *C'est incroyable* (It's incredible)!

Speaking of food, dinner was stupendous again. I had the succulent and savory vegetables with *brebis*, gnocchi with *confit* (preserves) of tomatoes and purple olives. *Merveilleux* (Wondrous)! Then, since they never asked me how I like my lamb, I had to send it back because it was raw. Medium rare is how I like it, not breathing. Many Europeans believe that most Americans like their meat well done, so they get into trouble when they assume without asking. Minutes later the young man from Lille brought me three tiny bits of medium, enough to taste. Next came a selection of goat cheeses before the lemon pie with homemade ice cream. Although they had a humidor full of select stogies, I grabbed one of my Montecristos and descended down to the bar. No one objected, the door and windows were open, so I fired away. Smooth and mellow, yet stimulating like a cup of espresso. *Bonne nuit*!

Provence, lundi 19 juin

Provence, Monday, June 19th

Because my days are so precious while traveling, I don't waste my mornings in bed except under very unusual circumstances. My natural alarm clock woke me early, and I enjoyed another delightful French breakfast on the terrace in a misty kind of morning that was trying very hard to clear up—still nice and cool. Said *au revoir* and off I drove 100 kilometers to Aix-en-Provence, the heart and capital of this blessed region. From there it was a straight shot 740 kilometers to the Capital City. My average speed was around 130 kilometers per hour, and surprisingly, I was rarely passed at that slow speed. Those big black BMWs and Mercedes must have been on vacation, you know, the ones that zoom up to within a foot of your bumper, flash their high beams, zip right by as soon as the fast lane is clear, and quickly disappear from sight. B*ien sûr c'est dangereux* (Damn right it's dangerous)! But this is France, and driving here is not a matter of drawing on your old laid-back habits from home. Never should you drive in the left lane unless you are passing a slower *voiture* (car) or truck or caravan or

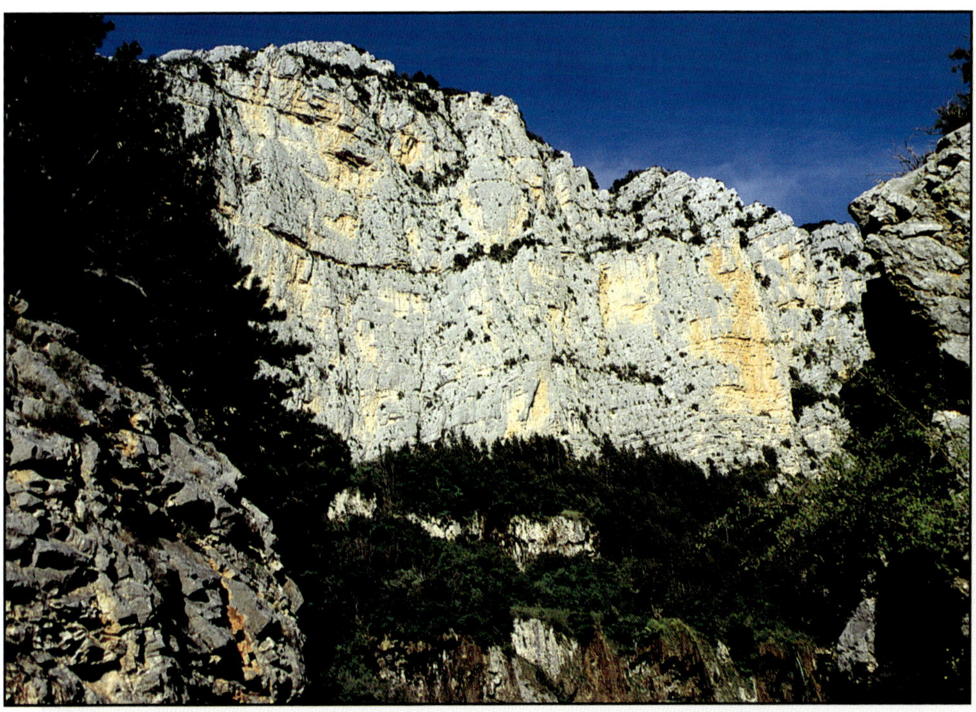

Spectacular cliffs of the Basse Alps of Provence.

bus or, and this is highly unlikely, a *moto*. *Motos* are those engines with two wheels propelling leather-clad thrill seekers who lunge forward to pass between two cars on the dotted lines going up to 140 miles per hour. *C'est fou, n'est-ce pas* (It's crazy, isn't it)?

Driving here is not for the meek and timid, and so what we end up with is a highway full of Indy racers, fools, and cupcakes who are lost and on vacation. But the *étranger* is not the only one who makes *des bêtises* (plays the fool) *avec de la connerie* (with damned stupidity). The locals can be just as frightening; especially when it comes to breaking little rules of the road that they feel are optional, like driving down a one-way street, or cruising along a sidewalk, or turning across parallel lanes to take a turn. They, especially Parisians, will park anywhere, but that is understandable in a city that has more cars than inhabitants (I would not be surprised if the French government started offering incentives to people not to drive in the city). There has to be ugly stone and metal barricades around the Places and Squares, otherwise Paris would be one big parking lot.

Driving into *La Ville* itself was kind of awesome as I managed to find the inner *Périphérique* (beltway circling the city), and could see many recognizable buildings including *La Tour Eiffel* and *Le Sacré Coeur*. At first, traffic was *fluide* (smooth), but that quickly changed to *bouché* (congested), bringing everything to a slow roll. With the staggering 90-plus degree temperature coming off the pavement (and no A/C in the "little red wagon"), the excess of pollution, and the fact that I was in a strange place altogether, I could only imagine the myriad problems that a breakdown would mean. Luck was on my side though, and even without a map, I managed to get off the *Périphérique* at the right place, taking me to *Place des Ternes*, where I found that one rare and precious space of pavement.

Jeanne-Marie was well, and we drank a Kronenborg 1664 together while Miriam and the Korean girl named Jenny prepared for dinner. I was invited to eat even though my arrival wasn't supposed to be until *minuit* (midnight), but I ended up eating a salad at my friend's Japanese-French *resto* just *en bas* (below). Later, I organized my things, showered, and reparked the car nearby. Remember that the best times to park a car here are around 19h30 after work and around 23h00 when people are leaving the restaurants. At any other time, good luck!

Paris, mardi 20 juin

Paris, Tuesday, June 20th

The crashing sounds of pots and pans woke me, and once I had drunk a pot of tea I called Ren and met him and his sister Robin at the well-known address of One rue Christine, where the restaurant of Jaques Cagnes can be found. What an excellent place in a perfect location—the apartment that is. I've never dined at Ren's celebrated neighbor's, but if you can afford it, I hear it is quite good.

Speaking of food, we had lunch at the *bar à vin* just on the other side, *en bas*, and it was light and tasty like *cuisine* in most wine bars. I had a salad of avocados and shrimp with coral sauce, smoked "salty" salmon from Norway on grilled bread with dill weed cream, and honey tart with walnuts, which was a very American-style dessert—copious, heavy, and sweet.

After the *déjeuner*, we took the *métro* to *Le Père Lachaise* cemetery and strolled around among Oscar Wilde, Gertrude Stein, Balzac, Appolinaire, Jim Morrison, and many other famous dead people. This somewhat grim place full of above

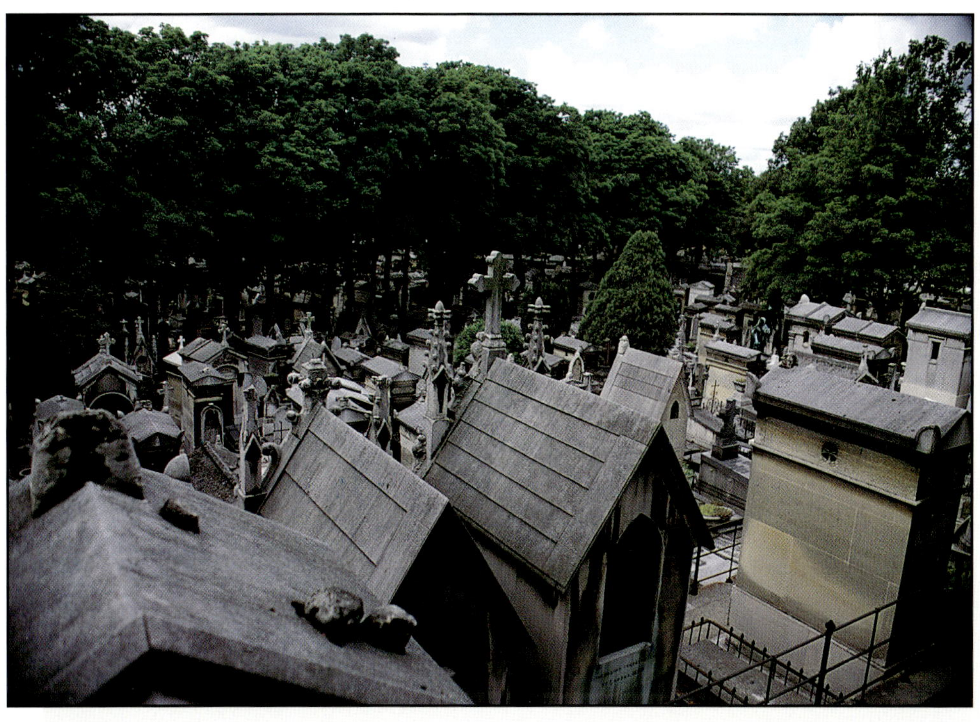

The city disappears when you're in Le Père Lachaise cemetery.

ground *sepultures* (tombs) with wild cats living in and around them is quite awesome because it envelopes you; you no longer realize that you are in a city of the living, but rather feel you have been transported to an otherworldly setting of tall trees on hilly terrain and perfectly carved stone boxes full of memories and bones. What an exciting place! You should definitley go there if you have a week or more in Paris. We separated, and I went home for a nap. Around six I went to the *Champs Elysées* to the Virgin Megastore for some CDs to send home, and to the English Pharmacy for American aspirin, which they did not have. When I returned for dinner, something slightly bizzare awaited me, a salad of mint leaves, avocado, melon, olive oil, and lemon juice. As the French would say, "*Il faut aimer*" ("You have to love it"). I love all of the ingredients, but not together. That night I talked to my sister, Bunny, and my brothers, A and Stevie, and they sounded like they were in the next room. That's French *technologie* and engineering for you! *Dors bien*! A *demain*!

Paris, mercredi 21 juin

Paris, Wednesday, June 21st

Got up at seven, had some yogurt, and read in my room before meeting Ren and Robin at the Louvre at precisely 10h45, at which time we were admitted for free because we had our museum director with us—Ren. We walked through the Richlieu wing, and for the first time, I saw the Apartments of Napoleon III, which truly bring back memories of a glorious past. Only the electric lighting where candles used to go was out of place, but, my goodness, how could they keep that many candles lit at one time? The sculptures on the *Rez-de-chaussee* (ground floor) were our favorite art objects of the day, because they were so lifelike, lacking only a little color.

We took coffee on the terrace of one of the museum's cafés and got our second winds so we could continue until lunchtime. Since she was flying home the next day, Robin got to choose the *resto*: the one near *Au Pied de Cochon* called *Pavillon Baltard*. We had salads with beets, ray with capers, *pintade* chicken with little caramelized onions and sliced roasted potatoes. This one was on me, so I ordered three champagnes with *crème de pêche* liqueur, the closest thing in France to an Italian Bellini, which is made from peach nectar. All around us the tables were full of people, dining outside in the pleasant summer air with umbrellas overhead. After our delicious meal, we checked out some of the local restaurant supply stores, which is always fun for those who cook, and ended up at the Marais, wandering around looking for a store never to be found. We did, however, find a store that had nice leather goods, so my friends bought gifts.

It had been several hours since we had eaten, *alors* it was my turn to pick the place for a snack—a *salon de thé*. We metroed it to the Concorde and walked towards the Madeleine church to a charming seventeenth-century tea room/pastry shop called *Ladurée*. Ren had *café Liegeois* ice cream, Robin had *café au lait*, and I had Ceylan Dovinia tea with milk and some of those delicious little cakes in the shape of gold bars called *financiers*. What a wonderful treat at 17h30 in the city on *rue Royale*! Then we piled into *Hermès*, and I bought some after-shave balm and a gorgeous ashtray with zebras on it for Mom. Hope she likes it. On my way home I stopped at Félix Potin to buy yogurt and beer, two staples for me in France.

I had dinner at home and then went to "*La Fête de la Musique*," a nationwide music free-for-all which takes place on the same day every year at almost every major intersection in every city and village in France. On a whim, we just hap-

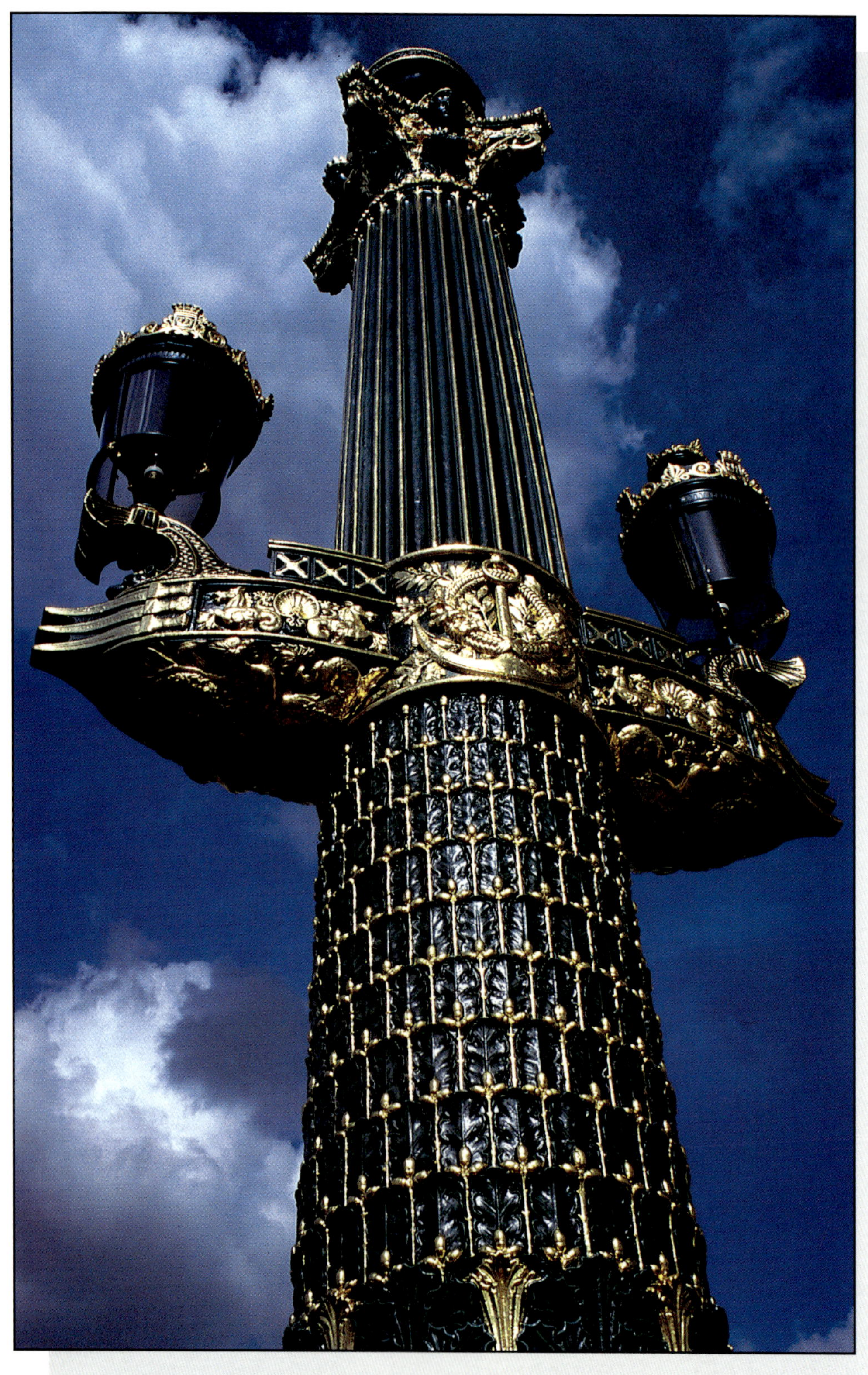

An exotic street lamp at the Place de la Concorde.

pened to end up at La Bastille where Joe Cocker and many other musicians played to an enormous audience of every kind of people you could imagine. The *fête* went on almost all night, and I can remember hearing the music at five in the morning from my window which opens on to *rue du Faubourg Saint-Honoré*. Once again, the people of France are united in a common celebration. *Salut*!

Paris, jeudi 22 juin

Paris, Thursday, June 22nd

Got up to a rather cool morning and had to wear a sweatshirt all day. On summer days like these, you have to remember that Paris is on about the same latitude as Montreal. Ren and I had lunch at *Chez Pento*, and it was quite good except their salads are very small. My salad was poached egg with *lardons* (smoked bacon chunks), and for *le plat principal* (the main dish) I had duck confit, which was sumptuous. For dessert we had a kind of *crème brulée* with sliced pears that was light and terribly rich at the same time; we skipped coffee, because next we were headed for the tea rooms of *La Mosquée de Paris*. On the way we walked by *La Sorbonne* and *Le Panthéon* to a *brocante*, or glorified garage sale, and I picked up a couple of colorful old ashtrays with alcohol and cigarette names that are now illegal to produce in this country. These *cendriers* (ashtrays) are becoming more and more valuable every day, and my collection is growing.

La Mosquée, a mosaic-filled Arab mosque that was built in the early 1900s, has a beautiful courtyard, an area designated for prayer, a gift shop which was under

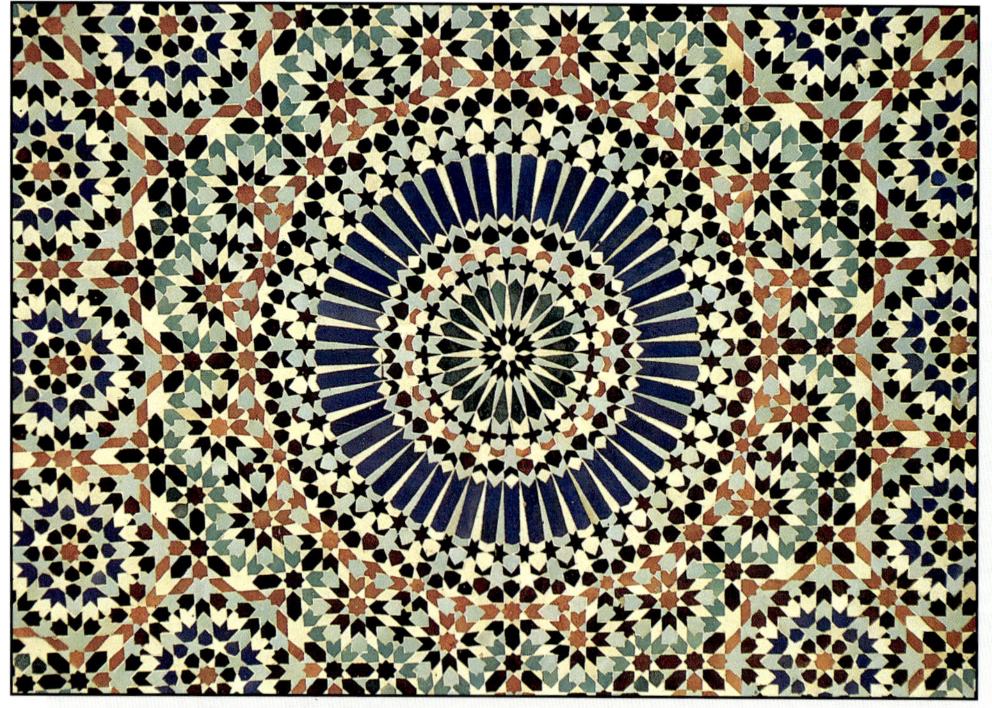

The mosaic wall in the garden of La Mosquée de Paris.

repair, and several wood-carved tearooms where you can drink hot, already-sweetened mint tea with Moroccan pastries. It is a trip away from France without ever leaving Paris. In the winter it gets packed, and cigarette smoke fills the air as the local population comes in out of the cold to sip from colorful glasses without handles and converse and people watch around brass tables.

Our next stop was the nearby *Jardin des Plantes* where we meandered through the gardens and continued along the *Quai Saint-Bernard* all the way along the left bank to *Saint-Michel*, where I caught the *métro* home. I was unexpectedly invited to have tea again with my Japanese friends as I was walking by their *resto*, and I accepted. I found out that they, like many of the French, go to Spain to vacation.

After dinner I went to see *Jefferson in Paris*, and I liked it mostly because it was about a man who fully appreciated French history and saw the genius in its culture. Yes, Thomas Jefferson brought back many ideas from a country that has always inspired those who search for some kind of ultimate experience of existence or way of life. I have to admire a man who laboriously kept a journal of not only the events of the day, but also of the novel discoveries that presented themselves in foreign lands to share with others who might not have had the chance to travel to those places.

Paris, vendredi 23 juin

Paris, Friday, June 23rd

Lazy morning! Did a little reading and some writing and then met Ren for lunch at the Hippopotamus down the street, a kind of glorified French steakhouse where you can order anything from a charcoal grilled burger to a *filet mignon* with *bernaise* sauce and fries. The food is generally good, made from quality ingredients, and the service is reasonably fast. I had a salad with baked *crottin* (sheep droppings), goat cheese and bacon, a New York strip with *bernaise* sauce, and a dessert called "*Ile Flotante*," which is meringue covered with *caramel* (burnt sugar), floating in a rich egg cream. Sinful!

Since the skies looked threatening, I left my "traveling companion" at the apartment, and we set out for the galleries near the Bristol Hotel, which offers quite possibly the finest accommodations in all of Europe. The galleries were full of expensive paintings by what I call "already-discovered artists"; therefore, we were just looking.

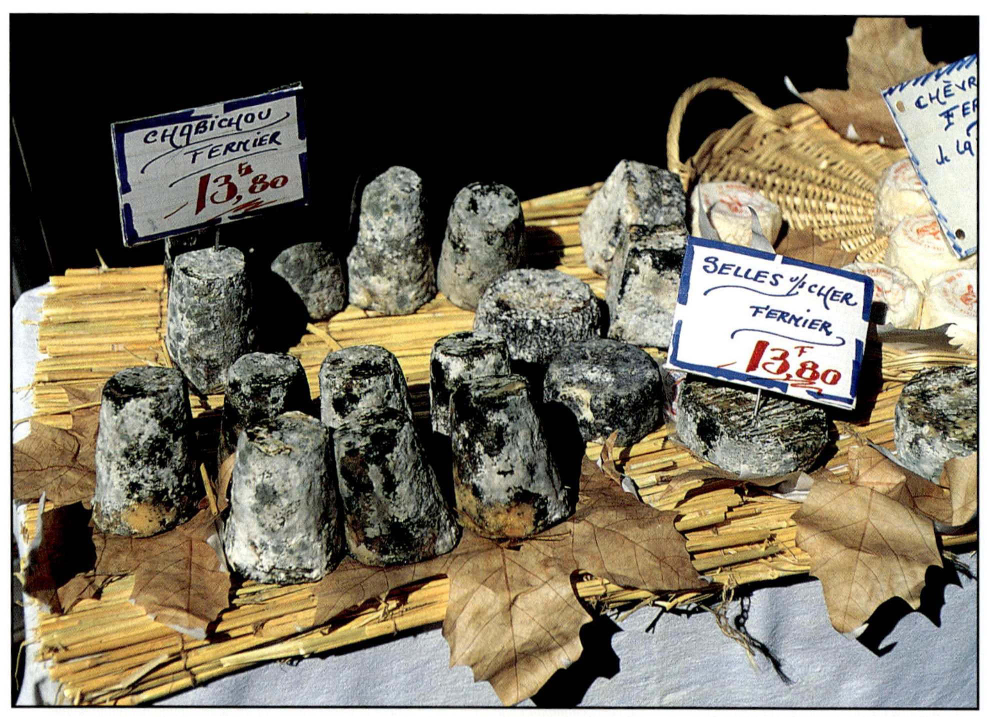

"Crottin" sheep's droppings cheese.

But speaking of "the finest," we decided to buy a gourmet take-home dinner at THE finest food store in the world where I worked, *Fauchon*! Covering two street corners and about seven stories high, *Fauchon* has been selling gourmet foods from around the globe for many years. You name it, they probably have it, from fresh exotic fruits like passion fruit and many others I can't even name to *foie gras* and caviar, from specially selected teas from around the world to fresh-baked pastries and artistic fruit-covered cakes, and from meat-filled *terrines* and broiled lobster tails with mayonnaise "to go" to Canadian maple syrup and peanut butter. *Fauchon* will even cook you a traditional Thanksgiving dinner, as it has done for so many expatriates for so many years.

My original memory of this "food heaven" dates back to 1984, when my friend Philippe brought me there to sample a few sweets. I was in awe, and since I was already working in a reputable *patisserie* in Grenoble, I could really appreciate what I was seeing. Then suddenly I had a wild idea. Why not ask to see if we could work in the *patisserie* there? The secretary smiled and said we should ask the gentleman behind her, because he was the *chef patissier*. It turned out that I was working for his old boss from years ago, and he immediately asked us when we could start work. Hallelujah!

The operation is nothing but class, and while I was there I witnessed the making of the New York Opera's one-hundredth-birthday present, a 100% chocolate replica of the Opera building itself! Ren and I selected some duck and rabbit *patès*, an apricot tart dessert, and combined that with a salad and ate royally and yet light. *Métro* home for some *dodo* (pronounced "doedoe," which means "sleep").

Paris, samedi 24 juin

Paris, Saturday, June 24th

Literally COLD today! I naturally woke up at a quarter to seven and drove my rental to Ren's in fifteen minutes flat. On a typical day that would have taken twice as long, but luckily it was *le weekend*, and Parisians *font la grasse matinée* (sleep in) on Saturdays. We drove out the *ancien* hamlet in the suburbs of *Port de Clignancourt* and were in the town of Compiègne at the crack of dawn, just in time for a hot cup of *café au lait* and a warm and crispy croissant. The town was bustling with activity as shopkeepers were preparing for the day, and we just walked around taking it all in on the cold and cloudy morn in the province of France.

Just as we reached the chateau gardens, which reminded me of Versailles because of the vastness, the sun came out, and suddenly we were uncomfortably warm in our sweaters and raincoats.

Lunchtime! We both had read about the *Rotisserie du Chat Qui Tourne*, so it was unanimous that we try it out. Since we were a little early for *le service*, a nice lady, probably the owner, served us *Kir Royals* in the old bar/library of the hotel until noon. I particularly enjoyed the little toasts and butter with caviar and shrimp and the hot pigs in blankets that we munched with our *apéros*. Once seated, I ordered the light green vegetable potage, chicken paprika with potatoes cooked on a wood fire, a broiled tomato, and apple custard pie for dessert. The service was excellent, but eating so copiously can make me feel a little sleepy, and there are only two cures: sleep, or a cup of "high test" *arabica*. We opted for the latter, which is almost to the human body what rocket fuel is to a jet airplane. *Ça va mieux* (That's better)!

Going back was a bit of a challenge with the unexpected traffic, so I let Ren out at Chatelet and drove up the *Champs Elysées* to the Place Charles DeGaulle Etoile, where I went halfway around the largest *rond point* (circular intersection) in France and turned down the Avenue MacMahon, finding a parking place in no time. *Je suis chanceux* (I'm lucky)!

That evening I headed to *Le Verre en Bouteille* wine bar and had a glass of Muscat de Rivesaltes, which is a sweet wine from the southwest of France, a region near the principle *ville* of Perpignan where I lived with a family during the summer of 1994. I'll never forget this charming ninety-year-old lady whose picture I took in a little nearby village called Villefranche de Conflent. She just talked and talked and I snapped pictures. Anyway, I had an excellent salad of duck, sausage, chicken, lentils, and all kinds of lettuces. Then I had another salad of *crottin de chèvre*, which was also tasty. Oops! I ate too much to have dessert. I've got to get my *profiterole*-fix soon. *Peut-être demain*! (Maybe tomorrow!)

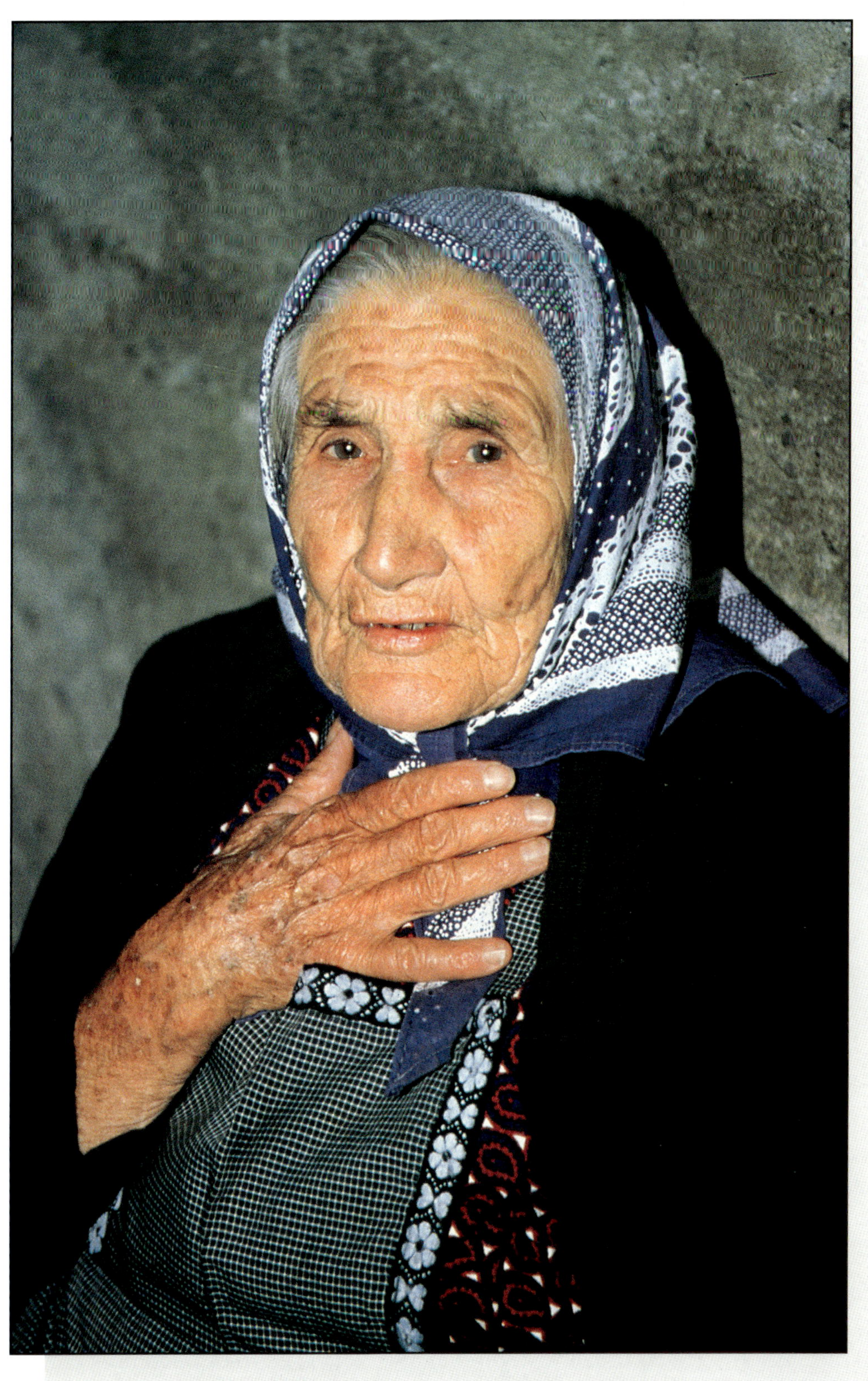

La dame de Villefranche de Conflent.

Paris, dimanche 25 juin

Paris, Sunday, June 25th

When I awoke there was a strange sensation of butterflies in my belly, because I hadn't seen her in what seemed like months. She would be landing about now at Orly on a flight from Marseille. My step was lighter, and I felt great as I left the shower to get dressed for a big day. Constance arrived around mid-morning, and when she walked in I just had to look for a moment but caught myself and gave her a hug. For the next couple of hours we brought each other up to date, and she informed me that she would be living in New York this winter. "Convenient," I thought to myself! I was really bitten by the bug, and had no means of hiding it.

We caught the *métro* to Odéon and walked to one of my favorite *restos*, Le Procope, which began hundreds of years ago as a place to buy that newly discovered roasted commodity called coffee. Eventually, it evolved into a place to eat, and is now the oldest restaurant in the City of Gourmet. *Kir Royals* were in order for me and my American friend from the South of France, and the waiter brought some mini meat *terrines* as *amuse-gueules*. Then we had terribly rich *rillettes de poisson* (fish rillettes), and baked chicken over noodles with a creamy sauce that was washed down by a 1988 *Bourgogne rouge*. Almost all French restaurants serve sherbets, and this one makes its own, so we enjoyed mango, pear, and strawberry *sorbets* with coffee.

It was a warm day, and with the low-flying clouds it looked like it could clear up or rain any minute, so we decided to walk to the *Ile Saint-Louis* and find a nice spot to just relax and watch the barges and *Bateaux Mouches* (small passenger steamers) go by. Constance has been to all the museums here, so we were not under pressure to mingle with the crowds to see priceless stretches of canvas with hardened pigments of oil carefully applied with horse bristles attached to long wooden handles. All we had to do was enjoy the rhythm of the city and the flow of its lifeblood through old walls of stone and under busy bridges of carefully laid rock and metal.

Later, we walked on and just took it all in: L'*Hotel de Ville* where the Mayor of Paris lives and works; Chatelet, the heart of the *métro* system; and up the *rue de Rivoli* to *Angelina*, a *salon de thé* opened in 1903 by the Austrian Antoine Rumpelmayer, where we stopped for the hot injection of creamy chocolate and whipped cream called *chocolat africain*, which is almost as thick as pudding, only twice as rich. Believe it or not the lady next to us not only drank all of her *choco-*

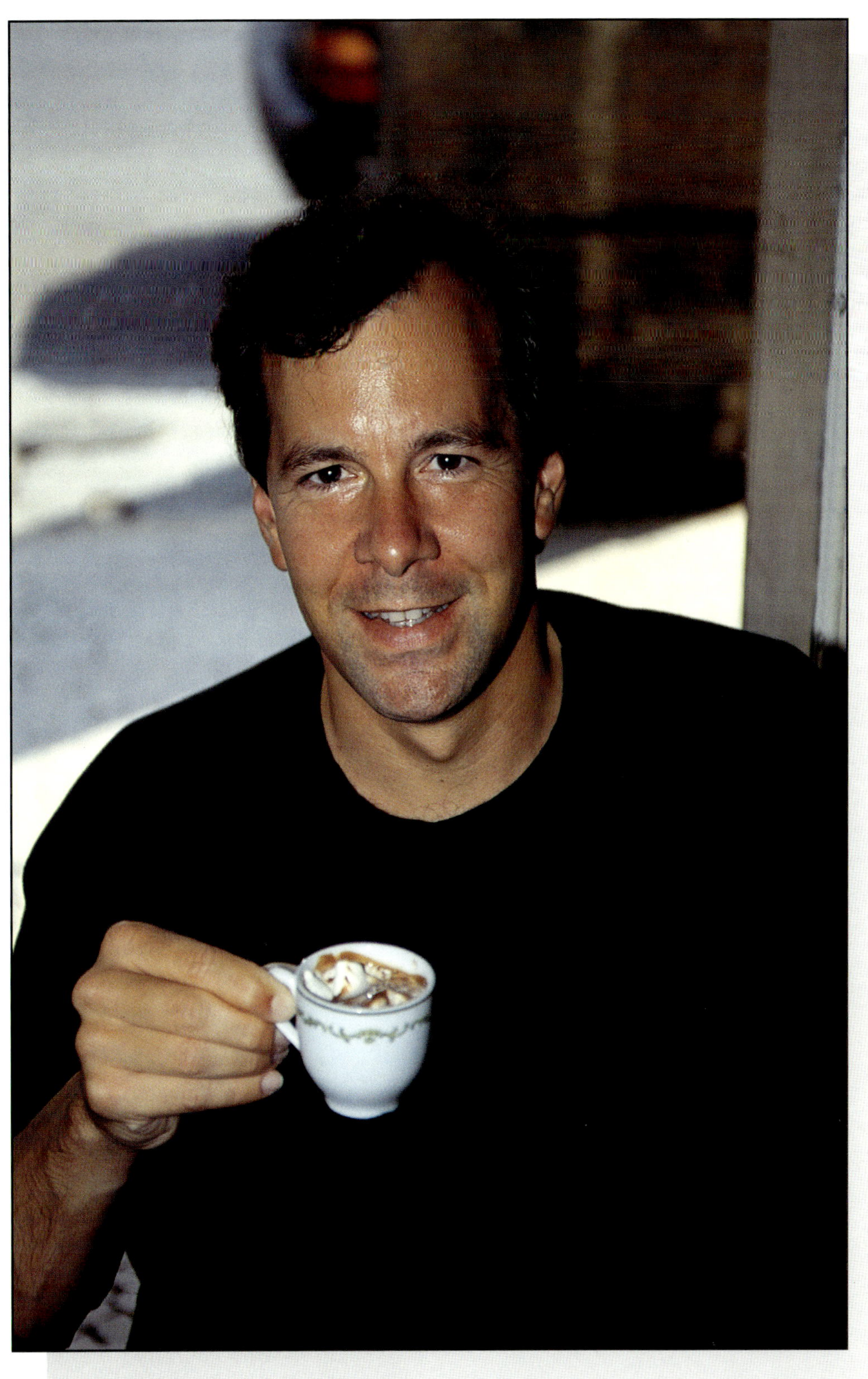

The author at Angelina's and his cup of chocolat africain.

lat africain but also ate an entire *Mont Blanc*—*meringue, chantilly,* chestnut cream purée, and powdered sugar for the summit. Even a "sweet tooth" like me was impressed.

We did some more walking, took a short nap, and then had dinner. The place was nearby, so we went *à pied* (on foot). The attractive waitress talked us into a rum, curaçau, and pineapple cocktail for an *apéritif,* a change of pace from all the wine-based *apéros* we normally drink. I ordered a bottle of Crozes-Hermitage, and it went splendidly with the tomato and mozzarella salad and *gigot d'agneau* (leg of lamb). Then I got my fix—*profiteroles à la vanille au chocolat.* Truly a decadent day in France! *Dors bien*! A *demain*!

Paris, lundi 26 juin

Paris, Monday, June 26th

Did my laundry while Constance was still asleep. We had our *petit dej* at Le Hoche, where three waiters came by the table to say "*Bonjour*." Had I become a "local" already, or were they just impressed by my gorgeous friend? *Les deux* (both)! Anyway, they are very kind to me there, and I often order French onion soup and endive and roquefort salad when I'm in the *quartier*.

Today, Constance wanted to get a little culture, so we went across the Pont Alexandre III to the Dome of Les Invalides where we saw the *tombeau* of Napoleon. When I bought our tickets to go inside, I jokingly asked the ticket lady if Napoleon was "in" today. We all laughed. Louis XIV, the Sun King, had the magnificent place built as a kind of hospital for veterans of war well before the days of Napoleon, and it has just been restored recently.

We had lunch at a nearby café: just-toasted *poilâne* bread with *gruyère* cheese, mushrooms, tomatoes, and artichokes. Then we walked to the Pont L'Alma

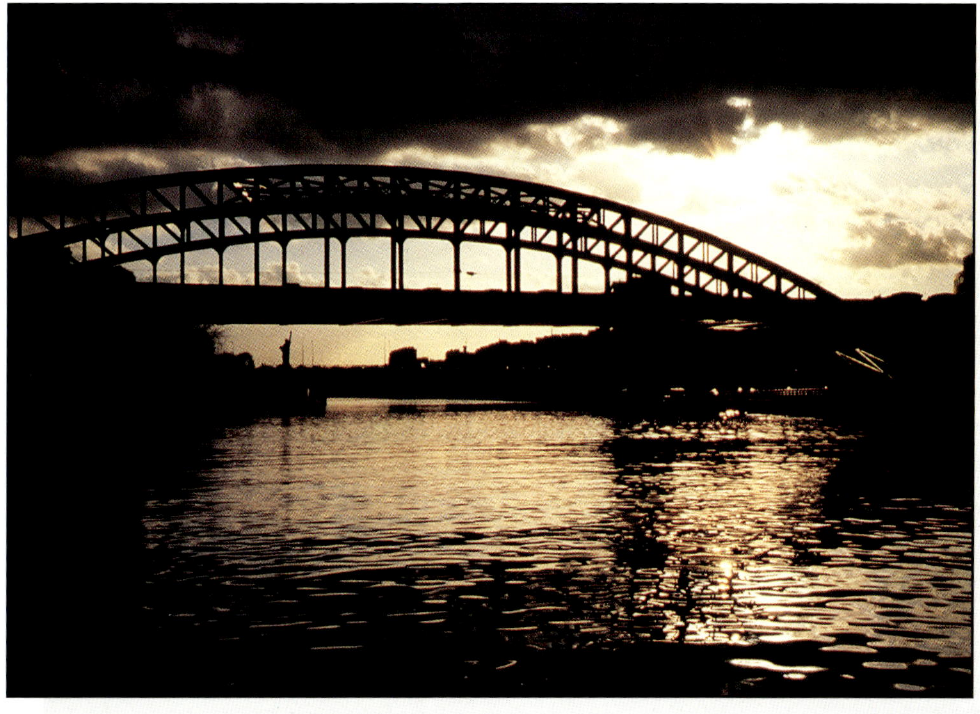

The Passerelle deBilly taken from a Beateau Mouche.

where we caught the *bateaux mouches*, another very romantic thing to do here in *gai* Paris. It's a unique way to see such an old city, because being on the Seine allows you to see many of the buildings, monuments, and churches without the bustling of cars and pedestrians, and from an angle that makes everything seem more ominous than it already is. I particularly liked the area of the Trocadero across from the Eiffel Tower, not very far from the original yet much smaller version of the Statue of Liberty. It was in this part of the river where I believe I got some good shots of the tower and nearby bridges with the sun peaking through the low-flying clouds.

Around seven, we walked back to the apartment to get ready for dinner at *La Ferme Saint-Simon* in the *septième* (seventh arrondissement). We had a delicious green salad, baked monkfish in a saffron vegetable sauce with mussels, and *mille feuille crustillant caramelisé aux fruits rouges*, which was crusty flaky pastry with caramel coating and fresh raspberries and strawberries and vanilla ice cream. Don't ever be surprised in a French restaurant if someone near you lights up a stogie and smokes it for a long time, filling a place of eating with filthy nasty air. I'm talking about a restaurant, for Christ's sake, where people pay a lot of money to eat. This is what happened to us at *La Ferme Saint-Simon*, and we shall never forget it. It's a shame too, because the food was pretty good and our waiter was tops, "Johnny on the spot," and friendly. Another thing I couldn't help but notice was that the posters had this gummy substance brushed over them to make them look like real paintings. There were six attractive Arab women, all wearing heavy perfume, sitting behind us, so you can imagine the mix of scent and smoke in the air. Speaking of air, we needed some, so we paid and made the long walk back but not before running into a friend of mine from North Carolina on the *Champs Elysées*. Mike, who is in the wine business, was in Paris with the Seagrams Company. Constance was impressed, I could hardly believe it, and Mike was a little shocked. We went our separate ways, and Constance whispered something in my ear as we rode the elevator to the second floor. *Bonne nuit*!

Paris, mardi 27 juin

Paris, Tuesday, June 27th

We made a little "*grasse matinée*," literally "fat morning," which means we stayed in bed until around 10h30. On the way to Ren's we each had a cup of liquid energy at Le Hoche and hailed a cab. I introduced my two friends, and we all sipped tulips of champagne and *crème de pêche* before walking across the street to an "every tea in the whole wide world" tea shop and *salon de thé* that serves lunch.

Since 1854, Mariage Frères has stocked hundreds of teas from all over the globe downstairs, and upstairs is the tea room and restaurant where we enjoyed a variety of *entrées*. My choice was the "snob salad"—*foie gras de canard*, smoked salmon, artichoke hearts, green beans, and all kinds of lettuces in a vinaigrette sauce. Understandably, everybody had a bite of my *foie gras*. I selected a nice smoky red bordeaux called Puy Caster to go along with our meals. We all shared each other's dessert, and the whole thing was a success even

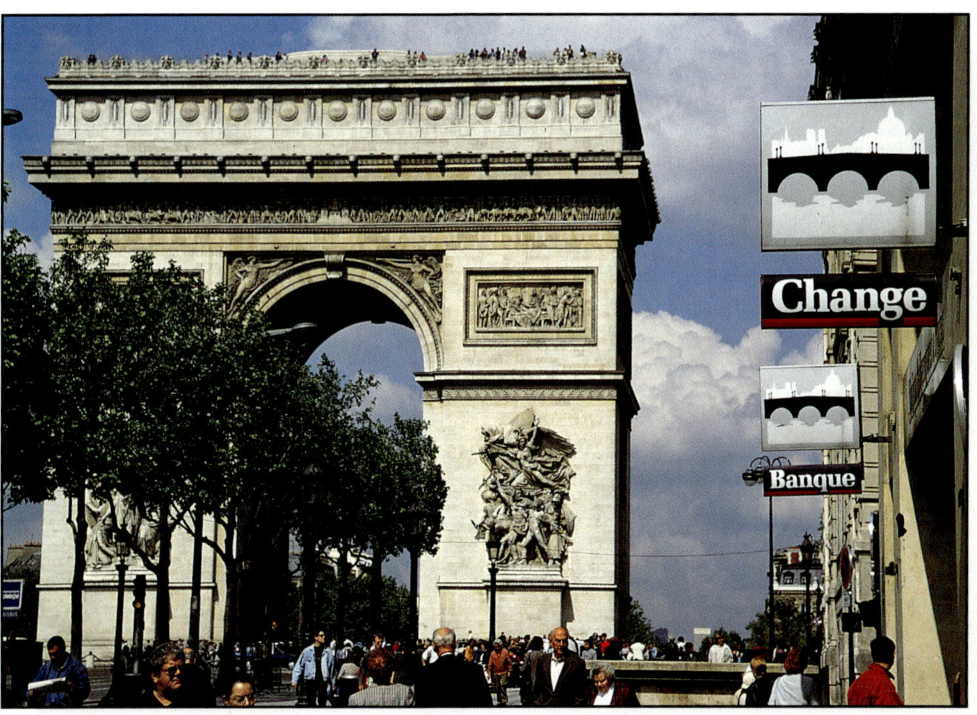

The Arc de Triomphe taken from the sidewalk of the Champs Elysées.

with a Nigerian tea, because Mariage Frères is the only restaurant in France that doesn't serve coffee, *naturellement*. Tea, though it does contain caffeine, just doesn't have that uplifting effect that coffee does, at least for me.

Unfortunately, Constance and I had to leave to return the "little red wagon" to SODEXA Peugeot, so we raced home in the *métro* to find her a little dirty, but untouched by *voleurs* (thieves). Courbevoie, a town located near *La Defence*, was our destination, but we took the wrong turn and had to ask for directions from a nice man. The second time around we got it right, and when I turned in the keys and papers, they didn't even bother to look at the car. Guess they trusted me. From there, we caught a bus to *La Grande Arche de la Defence*, where we took the *métro* back to the apartment to relax. Constance told me that Paris was fine for a few days but that the city was too crowded, too polluted, and too unfeeling for her to live here. That's exactly how I feel about New York, but not Paris. At least in Paris I can overlook the crowds and pollution, and as far as people go, I find Parisians among the friendliest I've ever met. It's true!

For dinner we wanted something simple, so we tried Chez Clement, the one on the *Champs Elysées*, and they've got an American concept going there called, "À *volonté*" or "All you care to eat." I chose the "*à volonté*" spit-roasted beef, spare ribs, and chicken with homemade mashed potatoes, and Constance had a salad and the *tartare* of salmon. She's *très française*!! Since we had enough wine with lunch we ordered a bottle of my favorite mineral water, Badoit, with its slight taste of minerals and small bubbles.

Needless to say, I left that *resto* with a full stomach *à l'Américain*, and so we decided to walk the feeling off. We walked down *Les Champs* and made it to La Concorde before turning back and calling it a night. Before *dodo*, I thought about my newfound friend who sort of has me hypnotized. Constance is so easygoing and fun to be with that I know I'm going to miss being with her in a few days. Is this a mere fling, or could it be the beginning of a hyper-long-distance romance? At least she would be in New York this fall. Just then, she came into the room and knelt by my bed and gave me a loving kiss, and I knew I would have *bons rêves* (sweet dreams) that night. *Dors bien mon petit chou* (Sleep well my little cabbage)!

Reims, mercredi 28 juin

Reims, Wednesday, June 28th

I awoke early to a cloudy cool day and Constance was already up and busy writing in her *journal intime* (diary). I'd like to know what's in there. After a typical continental breakfast, we headed to *La Gare de L'Est* to catch a train to the city where most of the kings of France were *coronnés* (coronated) with golden crowns: the beautiful capital of Champagne—Reims. A heck of a name to pronounce—the "m" is silent, not the "s." Only an hour train ride from Paris, Reims and the enticing vineyards of Champagne are a convenient and potentially intoxicating day trip, allowing you to be back in time for dinner.

From the station we walked towards the hotels and shops, and asked for directions to the *cathédrale*. It wasn't far, and when we arrived we just stopped and stared at the magnificent structure that has to be among the largest cathedrals in France. We went inside and marveled at the magnitude. I sat down and said a prayer, and we left.

All over this blessed country, people were preparing to have lunch, and we were no exception. After a few suggestions from a local shopkeeper, we worked our way back towards *La Gare* until we stumbled across one of the *restos* the lady had mentioned, *Le Continental*. We ordered the exact same thing—whole scallops successfully baked in a light buttery wine and cream sauce with strips of carrots, zucchini, and mushrooms, lightly browned on top, all bathing in a shell-shaped saucer—classic *Coquilles Saint-Jacques*! In France, fine restaurants leave on that orange stuff called "coral" that hugs half of the scallop, and I find it quite delicious with a pleasing texture. I heard that this orange part doesn't keep as long as the white meaty portion, therefore it is often removed in the U.S. I'm not sure what the truth is, so the verdict is still out on that. With our seafood we had baked cauliflower, mashed potatoes, and carrots. A *verre de champagne Pommery* complemented the hearty meal, which would have been perfect except for the fancy pear sorbet in the *Poire Belle Hélène*. Vanilla ice cream is what the original recipe calls for, and they should know that pear sorbet and chocolate just don't mix.

On the way back to the capital city I wondered why it was taking so long to get to Epernay, and just happened to ask a fellow passenger how long would the ride take, since it only took ten minutes coming the other way. *Une heure* (An hour)! In my disbelief I almost lost it, but avoided playing the ugly American by

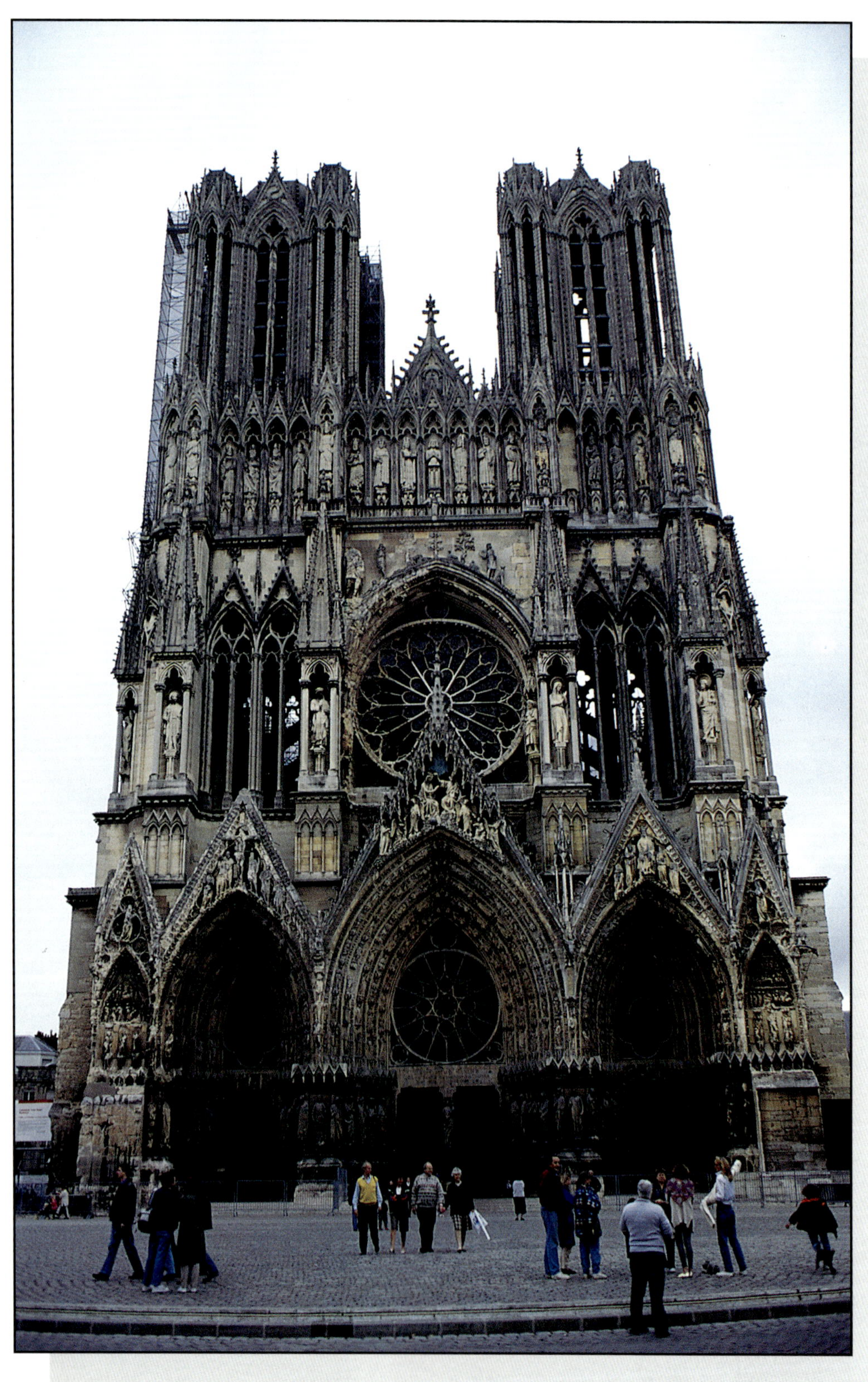

Kings and Queens were crowned in Reims at this cathedral.

not complaining about how ridiculous this slow piece of junk was. Besides, we had nowhere to be.

Not far from the *métro Mabillon*, near the *quartier latin*, is a little restaurant called *L'Arrosée*, one among many popular haunts in this newly in vogue part of town. The decor here is anything but new, but the paintings of Madec housed here in this temple of fine French cooking are somewhat modern yet colorful, giving the place a warm feel. In reality, the restaurant could have just opened yesterday, but those who work there shoot that theory all to hell. Service is smooth like clockwork, and the food is excellent, though no Michelin stars. No, *L'Arrosée's* star is shining in the hearts and minds of its employees and in those who partake in its joys of gastronomic pleasure. We started with *Americanos*, and with them they brought us thick yellow pancakes with popcorn shrimp inside for *amuse-gueules*. The waiter even brought us butter for our bread (Rare in France). Then for an entrée Constance had *jambon de Parme et melon* (Parma ham with Spanish melon) while I had the *Bisque de Homard et Langoustines aux épices doux* (lobster bisque with lobster dainties and sweet spices). Mine had chunks of lobster and *langoustines* in a thick, hot, creamy pumpkin-colored liquid born of the sea. We were both delighted. Our *Premier Cru Saint-Emilion* was just the thing to go with our *pavé de boeuf* (beef filet) with *bernaise* sauce, but I discovered from the owner, Michel Jean Audic, that the restaurant is named after a wine called *Chateau L'Arrosée*, which they serve as well. Dessert! Raspberries and strawberries with homemade vanilla ice cream and *coulis* of two fruits—how can that not be sublime unless you've eaten entirely too much; and then you need *le trou Normande*, which is a shot of 40% alcohol Calvados—the distilled anesthetizing nectar of fresh Granny Smith-type apples retaining their crisp tart fruity flavor and creating a veritable hole in your belly, enabling you to go on eating even though you're full. *C'était bon* (It was good)!

In the *métro* on the way back I felt like a human bomb ready to explode. Speaking of bombs, real ones are going off in this city and cops are everywhere, the *police nationale*, the *armée*, the *gendarmerie*, the secret police, you name it, and the *métro* is the most dangerous place to be. But today we were only victims of the culinary wizardry of this delicious country. (Women in France eat as much as, or more than, men. It's true! You see, men are always worried about the bill, the car, and the mistress, while women simply eat. A friend told me that and I thought it was funny, if not true.) *Bonne nuit*!

Paris, jeudi 29 juin

Paris, Thursday, June 29th

I kissed Constance good-bye, and she rode off in a taxi. What a sad moment, but I had work to do because Ray, a friend of Jeanne-Marie who lives in London, needed me to carry her bags to the *métro*. Shortly thereafter, I ended up at *Les Halles* to take pictures, but couldn't get anything to happen, so I met Ren and had lunch at the *Bar du Dragon* at the *rue du Dragon*, actually a local's dive not far from *Saint-Germain*. Just what I needed, a simple lunch of salad and toasted *Poilâne* bread with melted Cantal cheese. Ren and I caught up on the last few days. He talked about the great city and I talked about Constance. I not only couldn't get her off my mind, but didn't want to. Today she was in the same room. Tomorrow we would be an ocean apart. There was nothing I could do except wait, until I could hear her voice on the phone, wait for a letter, wait for the unknowns of a long-distance relationship.

For the rest of the balmy afternoon I shot pictures and walked through many *arrondissements*, which are sectors of Paris that begin in the center and uncoil clockwise all the way to twenty in the shape of a snail. They also tell you what number to add to 75000 to get the correct zip code for a person or place in a particular part of Paris. The air was thick and stagnant as I made my way to Montmartre and *Le Sacré Coeur*. I like to come here probably because I can see the city from such a height, and because I feel like part of the bustling activity with all the artists, sidewalk vendors, and tourists about. The church is absolutely amazing and can be seen from almost every tall vantage point in the city. To me, *Le Sacré Coeur*, sitting proudly on top of Montmartre, is almost as much of a symbol of Paris as *La Tour Eiffel*.

After walking so far, I just had to rest, so I caught the *métro* back to Ternes, dozing in the train's *strapontin* (foldout seat) most of the way home.

That night, Ren, his friend Alan, and I dined at an up-and-coming restaurant called *Campagne et Provence*, which serves nothing but creative fare. The *dorade* (sea bream) baked with *fenouil* (fenil) had a strong anise flavor, which I thought strange at first, but as I got used to the flavors of licorice the fish got better with every bite. Dessert was just as creative, as they presented me with a plate of fresh fruit on a sweet biscuit covered in white chocolate. Almost as good as safe sex!

We met some newlyweds at the restaurant who came along with us to One rue Christine to visit and drink grappa. I didn't realize how much I had drunk until

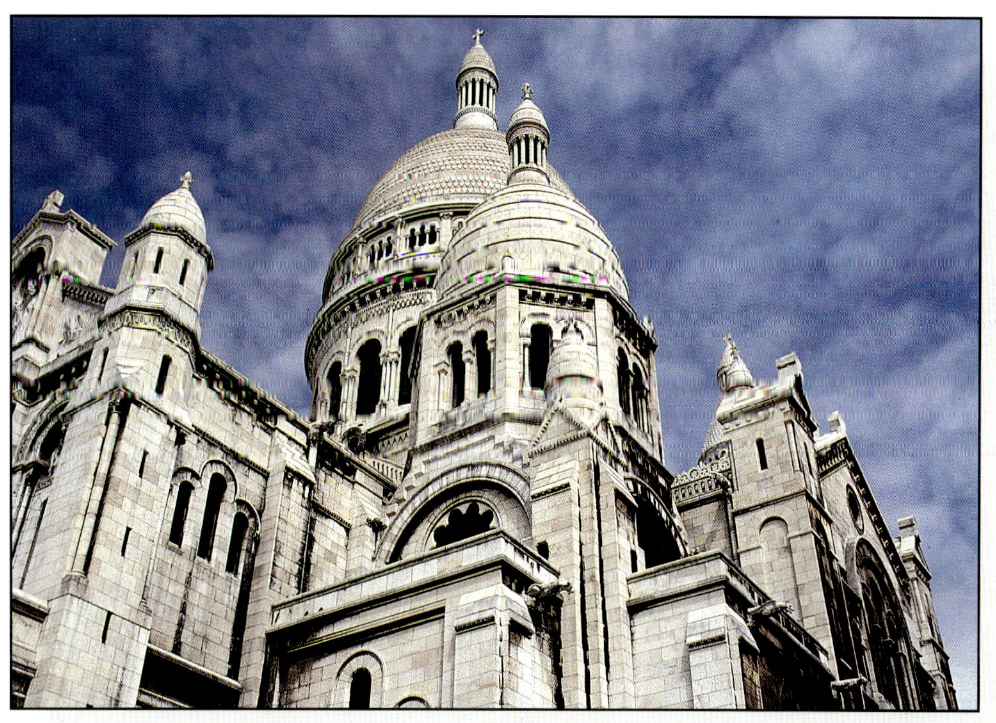

An unusal view of the Sacré Coeur (Sacred Heart Church).

my taxi driver and I got into a heated conversation about Americans being too lazy to learn foreign languages. It's partly true, but the real truth is that most Americans don't have to learn foreign languages to conduct their affairs, because English is the international language of business. Nevertheless, since we learn languages at school in the U.S., I blame our schools for not teaching us the two most important things about learning a foreign language—practical speaking and hearing. With those, you can communicate and actually interact with foreigners, but without them, you have nothing but endless rules of grammar and infinite verb conjugations, quite possibly rendering you deaf and dumb in that language for the rest of your life.

A *la prochaine*! (Until next time!)

Afterword

If you're luncky enough to go there.

My first *conseil* (advice) to you is to spend at least three nights in Paris and enjoy the grand cafés, the restaurants, the long walks along boulevards and tree-lined avenues, as well as down back streets of places like the Latin Quarter, the Seine, the monuments, the adrenalin that comes from the rushing cars, taxis, buses, and crowds of humanity, and the romance of just being a part of such a harmonious and seductive culture.

Next, I would suggest that you visit the provincial cities that attract you the most, taking the train for its comfort and scenery, and always making reservations in advance. You have many choices as to where to stay, from a cheap *chambre d'hôte* (room in a kind of farmhouse), to a four-star luxury suite with cold running champagne and room service. I prefer somewhere in between, but I should also mention that there are *relais* (country inns) in unexpected places that serve gourmet meals and oftentimes have rooms. There are *chateaux* from the twelfth century to stay in, and there are castles too. You have the choice, but always reserve in advance. You don't want to be caught in the middle of nowhere, seventy kilometers from the nearest Campanile (a chain of motel/restaurants), with no room in the inn.

Try new foods while you have the perfect opportunity, because chances are you'll like something that you would have a hard time finding outside of the big cities in North America. Sample some of the wonderful *aperitifs* offered, like the "*cocktail maison*," and ask about the wines of the region that you are in. Drink them! It may be your only chance. See if you like the hot black stuff in the mornings, and try tea with milk in the afternoon with one of the many delicious pastries, or have an ice cream concoction in the middle of the day without any guilt. Ride the *bateaux mouches*, and visit the Eiffel Tower. Go dancing at midnight at one of the many discoesque night clubs found from one end of France to the other. Drink the mineral waters, and see if you have a preference, but if you are saving your pennies then ask for *l'eau du robinet* (tap water).

Which reminds me, speak some French! Reach back to all those years of grueling study and try to say at least the simple things, like, *mercie* (thank you), *s'il vous plaît* (please), *je voudrais* (I would like), and point if you can't say it, *combien* (how much), *où est* (where is) and point to your map, and add all that to what's in your Berlitz and you'll be set.

Don't be shy in France. You can meet some really interesting people there from all over if you are willing to assert yourself. For singles this is mandatory. At least say hello or ask for directions. The point is, you only have so much time abroad, *alors,* don't waste it. Remember, you've got to be your very best self when you are separated from your home as a guest of strangers, so take advantage of this freedom to be the real you and live a little. Just take what your Mom and Dad taught you about good manners over there and you'll do just fine. Oh yeah—take your camera too! *Bon Voyage et A Bientot!*